CW00369853

POCKET
DIRECTOR

The
Economist
Books

POCKET
DIRECTOR

BOB TRICKER

The essentials of
corporate governance
from A to Z

THE ECONOMIST IN ASSOCIATION WITH
PROFILE BOOKS LTD

Profile Books Ltd, Registered Office:
62 Queen Anne Street, London W1M 9LA

First published by Profile Books Ltd
in association with
The Economist Newspaper Ltd 1996

Printed in Great Britain by
William Clowes Ltd, Beccles and London

A CIP catalogue record for this book is available
from the British Library

ISBN 1 86197 000 5

CONTENTS

INTRODUCTION

The success of every enterprise depends, ultimately, on the calibre of its directors and the effectiveness of its board. Management may run the business, but it is the directors who ensure that is being run well and in the right direction. Yet, around the world, there are different ideas on what the role of directors should be and about the structure and style of boards.

Pocket Director is a guide to the work of directors. It is aimed at both directors and managers, who are ultimately supervised by the board and who may themselves become directors one day. Although rooted in the theory of what the role of directors should be, it is based on sound practical knowledge of what directors really do and it emphasises ways of achieving board-level effectiveness. The ideas and insights are relevant to directors of all forms of corporate entity, including subsidiary and associated companies, family firms, non-profit companies and quasi-governmental boards, as well as to the directors of public companies listed on a stock exchange.

Although directors all have similar responsibilities in law, they play various roles in practice and make different contributions to their companies. They also face an increasing barrage of concerns, including rising expectations, increasing regulation and the threat of litigation. *Pocket Director* reflects this reality and enables those who are directors to maximise their contributions.

Part 1 sets the scene with six essays on what boards really do, directors' responsibilities, board structures and styles, and contemporary issues and conflicts facing directors. Cross-references in Part 1 refer to entries in Part 2, which is an A–Z of terms and ideas used internationally in discussing the work of directors and their boards. In this section words in small capitals usually indicate a separate entry, thus enabling readers to find other relevant information (though they should note that abbreviations such as CEO and IBM are also in small capitals). The appendixes in Part 3 contain details of some of the reports and guidelines referred to in Parts 1 and 2, useful checklists for directors, case studies and sources of information.

Pocket Director is informative yet lively, showing that the director's work is stimulating, challenging and creative – a far cry from the set of dry legal responsibilities described in some other books. The successful director needs a tough-minded ability to think strategically, to communicate effectively and to act decisively, with integrity. The successful manager who may not yet be a director needs to know what the roles of the directors of the business are – and how they are likely to exercise them.

Part 1
ESSAYS

DIRECTORS' ROLES

What do company directors do? According to conventional wisdom, directors set the strategic direction for their companies. That is why they are called directors, after all. They appoint top management and monitor performance. Directors think rationally. They are experienced, analytical decision-makers. Directors always put the interests of the company ahead of their own. Reality suggests otherwise, however, as anyone who has ever served on or, as a manager, has had contact with a board of directors will know. Companies, and the boards of directors that govern them, can be strikingly different.

What directors do...

In some cases a board is intimately involved in the day-to-day running of the business, formulating its strategy, agreeing plans, allocating resources, monitoring its results and controlling its performance. In other cases a board may do little more than appoint the chief executive and rubber-stamp the proposals that come forward from management. Much depends on the governance power-base of the company and the structure and style of the board. Sometimes a board can be an administrative convenience, a legal requirement for approving decisions taken elsewhere in the organisation. Such a board might not even meet formally. But it is important to remember the work of a board can change the circumstances facing the company.

...and what they need to do

Figure 1 on the next page provides a simple framework for thinking about the work of directors.

Directors need to look outwards, beyond the company, seeing the business in its competitive, commercial context. They must also look inwards at the component parts of the company. They need to be able to focus on the future of the business in both the medium and the long term; and

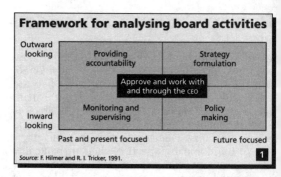

Framework for analysing board activities

	Outward looking		
	Providing accountability		Strategy formulation
		Approve and work with and through the CEO	
Inward looking	Monitoring and supervising		Policy making
	Past and present focused		Future focused

Source: F. Hilmer and R. I. Tricker, 1991.

1

they must concentrate on the present position and recent performance.

In strategy formulation the board looks ahead in time and externally in direction, seeing the firm in its strategic environment. Then strategies need to be translated into policies that can guide top management. At the same time the board needs to monitor and supervise the activities of the executive management, looking inwards at the current managerial situation and recent performance. Finally, accountability involves looking outwards and reflecting corporate activities and performance to the shareholders as well as other stakeholders with legitimate claims to accountability. (See ACCOUNTABILITY, MONITORING MANAGEMENT and STRATEGY FORMULATION.)

The literature of management is replete with two by two matrices. The only excuse for adding yet another is this one's claim to comprehensiveness: if the directors are looking internally and externally, in the past, present and future, there is nowhere else they can look.

Finding a balance

Central to a board's work is the need to ensure that the company has the right leadership. This is shown in the centre of the quadrant. A board has to appoint, monitor and, if necessary, replace the chief executive officer (CEO). Moreover, the directors need to determine how much responsibility they want to delegate to the CEO and top management and how much they want to reserve for themselves. Boards vary considerably in the allocation of activities between the chief executive and the board as a whole.

A board also faces choices on how it allocates time and effort between the four activities. Asked about the appropriate focus of attention between the four quadrants, many directors recognise the need for more attention to the strategy formulation, top-right quadrant, but admit that short-term business pressures tend to pull the focus towards executive monitoring and supervision in the bottom-left quadrant.

Figure 1 contains a further insight into board-level activities. The left and right sides of the matrix contain fundamentally different types of activities, as shown in Figure 2. On the right, strategy formulation and policy-making are activities that contribute to the future performance of the firm, whereas those activities on the left – supervision and accountability – are about ensuring and reporting conformance to policies and plans.

The two primary functions of the board

Outward looking	Providing accountability	Strategy formulation
	CONFORMANCE	PERFORMANCE
Inward looking	Monitoring and supervising	Policy making
	Past and present focused	Future focused

Different roles for different directors

Traditionally, company law has not distinguished different types of directors: all directors carry the same responsibilities, whether they are executive directors or non-executive directors, whether they have some interest in the company or are totally independent outside directors. All are responsible, individually and together, for ensuring that the company is properly governed, in line with the law and for the benefit of the shareholders as a whole.

There have been suggestions recently, however, that the role and responsibilities of non-executive directors are beginning to be differentiated from those of executive directors. The findings in the 1992 AWA case (AWA Limited *v* Deloitte, Haskins, Sells and others) in Australia recognised that non-executive directors were not in the same position to know and take action as executive directors. The proposals in the Cadbury Report in the UK on the financial aspects of corporate governance also emphasised the role and significance of non-executive directors. Some believe that such developments would enable a court in the future to separate the responsibilities of non-executive and executive directors.

Legal responsibilities aside, there is no denying that different directors can and do make quite different (and often changing) contributions to their boards.

Performance and conformance
The work of a board can usefully be separated into two areas. First, in the performance role, the directors focus on strategic and policy issues for the future, setting the corporate direction and contributing to the ongoing performance of the business. Second, in the conformance role, the board supervises management, ensuring that the company is conforming to predetermined policies, procedures and plans and is achieving the performance required, as well as demonstrating proper accountability for the company's activities.

These roles require much discussion, deliberation and review, to which the contribution of individual directors is crucial. Twelve different roles have been identified, covering the principal inputs that directors can make to their boards. Most directors will play more than one role and their roles may well change over time and according to the issues before the board, but because of potential conflict, any one director is unlikely to play all roles.

Three of the six performance roles – wise man, specialist and window-on-the-world – are concerned with contributing knowledge, expertise and external information. The other three – figurehead, contact person and status provider – are more concerned with networking, adding status and representing the company. (See PERFORMANCE ROLES.)

The six conformance roles – judge, catalyst, supervisor, watch dog, confidante and safety valve – are concerned with ensuring that the company follows the policies, procedures and plans the board has determined, with satisfactory results. (See CONFORMANCE ROLES.)

Directors' duties and responsibilities

The principal responsibility of directors is to the members of the company, that is the equity shareholders. In almost all jurisdictions two basic ideas underlie directors' duties: that they act with probity; and that they exercise reasonable care, diligence and skill.

Honesty, integrity and candour

The primary duty of a director is to act honestly in good faith for the benefit of all of the shareholders, giving them equal, sufficient and accurate information on all issues that could affect their interests. Directors may not treat the company as though it exists for their personal benefit. Even in the case of the "closed" company, in which the owners, the directors and the management are the same people, the company is an independent entity and the rights of other parties, such as the creditors and the state, need to be respected by the board.

A director must not make a secret profit out of dealings with the company. Any such interests must be disclosed to the board. For example, if a director is associated with another company whose tender for a major contract is being considered by the board, this interest must be disclosed. The board might decide that there is no problem and ask the director to refrain from comment or voting on the matter, or even ask the director to leave the room while it is being discussed. Having declared an interest, directors would be wise to ensure that it has been minuted, in case it is raised in the future.

Insider trading, that is dealing in the shares of a quoted company on the basis of information that is price-sensitive and obtained in a privileged way as a director, is improper. Indeed, in almost all jurisdictions it is now a criminal offence, although in some places prosecutions have been relatively few because of the difficulties of obtaining reliable evidence.

In practice, this fiduciary duty to act in the interests of the company as a whole can prove quite difficult for directors. Take a typical example. Warren Bishop was nominated by the finance house for which he worked to serve on the board of a start-up company. The finance house had subscribed for 25% of the equity capital plus a major loan, convertible to equity in the future. Mr Bishop attended board meetings assiduously and followed the development of the company's business with great care. He fully appreciated the cash-flow difficulties that faced the company in its first few years. But he found himself in a difficult situation. As a director, concerned for the shareholders as a whole, he knew the company must have additional funds to fund working capital. As a representative of the finance house, however, he did not feel able to recommend that they risk additional funds, even though that would put the future of the company in jeopardy. Such dilemmas frequently occur where there are representative or nominee directors. (See REPRESENTATIVE DIRECTOR.)

Nevertheless, boards must take decisions in good faith for the common good of all shareholders. Commonwealth-based company law tends to allow directors to determine the best interests of them all as a whole, subject to the right of appeal to the courts. Directors of companies incorporated in most US states owe specific duties to minority shareholders.

Care, diligence and skill

A further overall duty imposed on directors, by statute and case law depending on the jurisdiction, is the duty to exercise reasonable care, diligence and skill in their work as directors. The interpretation of what constitutes reasonable skill and care varies among countries and has been changing over time.

In the past, for example, in the UK a directorship was not an onerous task. An occasional meeting, a few questions, an expression of interest and support, for a fee and, perhaps, a lunch, was often all that was required. This has now changed. Legal actions have been brought against companies, boards and, in some cases, individual directors alleging negligence, abuses of power or infringement of the rights of minority shareholders. Moreover, the courts have extended their expectations of what can reasonably be expected of a director.

Directors do not need to be lawyers or accountants to fulfil their legal responsibilities, but it is wise for them to be briefed on such matters to ensure that they know when to seek advice. Obviously, directors with professional qualifications can reasonably be expected to act with the skill and care of experts in their fields. But more and more is now expected of all directors, including those who do not have professional qualifications.

The board of directors is the overall decision-making body in the modern corporation. The directors carry the ultimate responsibility for everything the company does. Yet most directors, and there are millions of them around the world, have never had any formal training for their work. The majority are unaware of the growing body of knowledge that is now available about the work of directors, board-level effectiveness and the exercise of power of the modern corporate entity – what is now called corporate governance. There are similarities to the position of managers in the 1950s, before the growth of management training, management theories and business schools.

The standard of professionalism expected of directors around the world is significantly higher than a few years ago and rising. Courts are increasingly prepared to act if fraudulent or negligent behaviour by directors is alleged, or where there seem to be abuses of power by directors or infringements of minority rights. Business decision-making, however, involves making judgments and taking risks, and it is not the role of the courts to second guess commercial judgments made by directors, even though with hindsight they turn out to have been misguided.

Corporate effectiveness

What has been said so far is, broadly, relevant to the directors of all companies, but particularly those of public, listed companies. The basis of power in some other types of company can influence the basis of corporate governance and affect the responsibilities of directors.

Subsidiary and associate companies Directors of companies operating within groups – including wholly and partly owned subsidiaries, associated companies in which another company holds less than a controlling but nevertheless a dominating interest, and companies in strategic alliances – can find themselves in special circumstances.

Difficulties can arise if control over the group of companies is exercised through group-wide organisation and management control systems, rather than through the governance structure of each company. If the subsidiary is wholly owned, whether a decision is made through group organisational channels or through the governance structures may not matter much. Where there are outside, minority interests in a company, directors can face problems.

Consider an example. John Write was the managing director of a subsidiary company in a British group of diverse companies. The group had acquired his company from family interests some years earlier. About 18% of the shares of the subsidiary were still in the hands of family members. Mr Write realised that he had a duty towards these minority shareholders, but he also had a duty to the group as the major shareholder. More significantly, he was also an employee of the group which determined his remuneration and promotion prospects. All went well until the group head office decided on a change of strategy. The products of the subsidiary company, it was felt, were in decline and, rather than invest in product innovation, it was decided to treat the company as a "cash cow", deny it further investment and "milk" it in order to start up new ventures elsewhere in the group. Mr Write faced a dilemma: how could he reconcile his duty to the group, which employed him, and his duty to the minority shareholders of the subsidiary company, of which he was a director?

Strategic alliances In recent years alliances between companies have become widespread as a strategic response to product innovation, procurement, production, marketing, or financing needs. Directors of companies created in such situations can face some similar conflicts.

For example, Jean Williams was appointed by her company, a major US telecommunications organisation operating around the world, to the board of a joint-venture company whose shares were held 60% by her company and 40% by a Japanese group. The strategic alliance had been formed to manufacture electronic components in Thailand and China, using technology developed by the Japanese and the distribution channels of the US group. Unfortunately, after three successful years of operation, the Japanese partners felt that changes in manufacturing technology and in the market necessitated a fundamental change in the product pricing structures, which would have been to the detriment of the US owner. Ms Williams was in a difficult position. As a director of the associated company she knew that her duty was to this company and both of its shareholders. She could see the Japanese firm's point of view but she also had a loyalty towards the US company that employed her. Her difficulties were compounded by the threat of litigation by the Japanese firm if she disclosed information given to her as a director of the associated company to her American bosses. In the event the company was wound up.

Family companies In the family company another set of issues can arise for directors. Although ownership may remain in the hands of the founder and, perhaps, members of the immediate family and a few loyal employees, corporate governance is often dominated by the founder-manager. Inside directors are closely related to the founder and outside directors, if they exist, have usually been invited to add knowledge, skills and experience that is not otherwise available on the board. But on succession real problems can arise, particularly if inheritance has split the shareholding between family members who are still involved in management and those who are not.

Consider another example. A prosperous family company, manufacturing and retailing furniture in the mid-west of the USA, was run by the son and daughter of the founder, each of whom held 25% of the shares. Another 25% of the equity was held by their brother, a lawyer in San Francisco, and the remainder by a cousin who lived in France. The family members with executive positions naturally wanted to enhance their remuneration and benefits, arguing that it was their work that was producing the performance. The outside shareholders, however, resented the rewards being taken by the incumbent executive directors. "Why should they give themselves these fancy cars, high salaries and expensive trips abroad?" they asked. "The original directors never spent that much on themselves." Another problem for the directors arose when other family members expected early promotion to top management posts, whereas the business had reached the stage of growth and complexity which desperately needed executives with professional qualifications and experience that the sons and daughters of the family lacked. The power struggles at board level became a particular problem for the chief executive, who was also the chairman. He tried to resolve them by appointing independent outside directors to advise him, but could not avoid a family feud.

Corporatised and privatised companies In recent years there has been a trend throughout the Western world of corporatising (making state-owned businesses more like companies in the private sector) or privatising (selling off all or part of the business to the private sector) such state entities as power, water and transport utilities and telecommunications companies.

Directors of such companies face unique problems. In the corporatised quasi-government entity there is the question of who should appoint the directors since the state remains the sole shareholder. Political issues can arise; for example, in privatised companies should the state retain a voting majority of the equity or a "golden share", to ensure that the strategically important interests of the country do not fall into the wrong hands? How is performance to be determined since, in many cases, there remains a degree of monopoly in the supply of services? Then there is the matter of social costs. In many utilities, if market forces were to be given a free rein, consumers who are poor or who live in remote areas might suffer. Mechanisms to regulate market prices are often introduced. All these issues affect the responsibilities of directors of such quasi-government companies.

Non-profit corporate entities Finally, there are the directors of non-profit enterprises, sometimes incorporated as companies limited by guarantee. It is possible that directors of such enterprises will also be bound by legislation designed to regulate charities and other non-profit entities. They might also find themselves in the position of trustees. However, the fundamental duties to act with honesty, integrity and candour, and to exercise care, diligence and skill still apply. But, by definition, non-profit companies lack the profit basis for measuring performance. Consequently, a particular challenge to the boards of such entities is to determine the precise mission of the corporate entity and the criteria by which success is to be measured. Balancing the pursuit of multiple objectives, in both the long and the short term, can be difficult.

BOARD STRUCTURES

The board of directors seldom appears on the organisation chart of a company, yet it is the ultimate decision-making body. Few of the standard reference works on management and organisation draw a distinction between the work of management and of the board: yet that distinction is fundamental to understanding the work of directors. The role of management is to run the enterprise and that of the board is to see that it is being run well and in the right direction.

Typically, management operates as a hierarchy. Although the organisation may not be a neat pyramid, there is an ordering of responsibility, with authority delegated downwards through the organisation and accountability upwards to the ultimate boss, on whose desk "the buck stops". By contrast the board should not operate as a hierarchy. Each member bears the same duties and responsibilities and together the members need to work as equals, reaching agreement by consensus or, if necessary, by voting.

A useful way of depicting the interaction between management and the board is to present the board as a circle superimposed on the hierarchical triangle of management, as in Figure 3.

This model can be applied to the governance

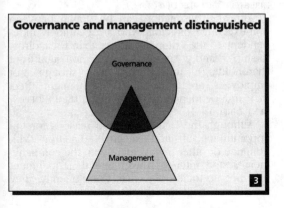

Governance and management distinguished

Governance

Management

3

of any corporate entity, private or public, profit-oriented or non-profit. The circle and triangle model is a powerful analytical tool and has been used to plot complex group inter-relationships, demonstrating in whose hands power actual lies, in a way that traditional organisation structure diagrams cannot.

The significance of board structure

What is the most appropriate structure for a board of directors or the governing body of a non-profit entity? How big should the board be? What proportion of the directors should be managers in the firm? What proportion should be outside, non-executive directors? Should the chairman of the board ever also be the chief executive?

Board structure is at the foundation of board activity; board membership (the abilities, affiliations and attributes of the members) provides the driving force; and board style (the processes, powers and politics of the board) produces the effectiveness.

At its simplest, board structure distinguishes between directors who hold management positions in the company and those who do not. Those with management positions are often referred to as executive directors and those without such positions as non-executive or outside directors. (See EXECUTIVE DIRECTOR, NON-EXECUTIVE DIRECTOR, OUTSIDE DIRECTOR.)

A further distinction can be drawn between non-executive directors who are genuinely independent of the company (other than their directorship and, perhaps, a non-significant shareholding) and those who, though not employees, are in positions which might affect their independence and objectivity. (See INDEPENDENT DIRECTOR.)

Although there may be good reasons for the appointment of non-executive directors with nominee or other involvement with the company, their vested interests mean that their judgment may not be totally objective. Consequently, they would not meet the check and balance requirements of audit, nominating or remuneration committee membership. (See AUDIT COMMITTEE, NOMINATING COMMITTEE, REMUNERATION COMMITTEE.)

Structural options

In the Anglo-American traditions of corporate governance the unitary board is the norm, that is a single board made up of executive and non-executive directors in whatever proportion is thought appropriate. In the continental European model there is a two-tier board in which an upper board supervises the executive board on behalf of stakeholders.

The all-executive board

In the all-executive board every director is also a managerial employee of the company. Many start-up and family firms have this structure, with the founder, close colleagues and other family members all working in the business as well as being

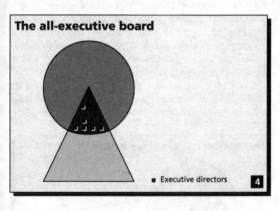

The all-executive board

■ Executive directors 4

members of the board. The boards of some subsidiary companies operating in groups also choose the all-executive board, which is, in effect, the top management team of the business with no outside members. The boards of major Japanese companies are large and effectively comprise executives from the company. (See JAPANESE CORPORATE GOVERNANCE.)

The majority-executive board

In the evolution of companies and their boards, non-executive directors get appointed to boards for a number of reasons. Sometimes, in a developing private company, the executive directors feel the need for additional expertise, knowledge or skills to supplement their own. Non-executive directors can also be appointed to be nominees of those investing equity or lending money to the business, or to secure relationships with suppliers, customers or others in the added-value chain of the business. Another reason can be succession in a family firm, when shareholdings are split between branches of the family.

A potential problem of a board which is dominated by its executive directors is that they are, in effect, monitoring and supervising their own performance. One solution, other than appointing more independent non-executive directors, is for the chairman to agree with newly appointed executive directors what is expected of them. Executive directors have to wear two hats, one as the manager of a part of the business, the other as a director responsible for the governance of the company. The important thing is not to be wearing the manager's hat in the boardroom.

Until recently most public companies listed in the UK had a majority of executive directors. The conventional wisdom was that "non-executive

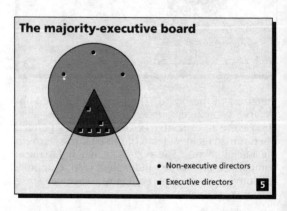

The majority-executive board

● Non-executive directors
■ Executive directors

5

directors play an important part; there should be more than one otherwise he or she would have no power or influence (the threat of resignation would carry little weight); about a third is right but never as many as half because the company needs to be in the hands of those who are running it." Exceptions were banks and insurance companies. But attitudes are changing. In the UK the Cadbury Committee report on the financial aspects of corporate governance has been influential in emphasising the importance of independent non-executives. Consequently, the proportion of non-executive directors in British public companies has been increasing and the typical major company now has a non-executive board membership approaching 50% or higher.

The majority non-executive board

The practice of leading public companies in Australia and the USA is to have boards with a majority of non-executive directors. In many such companies the outside directors heavily outnumber the inside executive directors. Some argue that if the outside members dominate the board, the governance process has really ceased to be a unitary board but has moved towards the power structure of a two-tier board.

Two challenges are often thrown at outside directors: that they cannot know as much about

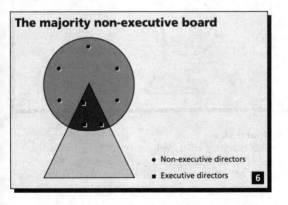

The majority non-executive board

● Non-executive directors

■ Executive directors

6

the business as executive directors, and that the time they can devote to the company's affairs will not be sufficient. The answer to the first issue is simple: outside directors do not need to know as much about the business as the executive directors; they need to know enough to make their unique contributions. The second is an issue to be discussed before accepting the invitation to join the board. The induction checklist for directors (see Appendix 5) should prompt all the necessary questions.

The two-tier board
In the two-tier model the members of the supervisory board are totally separate from the top management team. This is the basis for corporate governance in some continental European countries. (See GERMAN CORPORATE GOVERNANCE and the Metallgesellschaft case study in Appendix 6.)

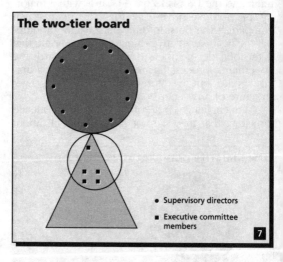

The two-tier board

- Supervisory directors
- Executive committee members

7

Board size
The number of members on a board can have a significant bearing on its effectiveness. The chemistry of interpersonal relations at board level can be sensitive and sometimes volatile. Directors

(with the exception of those appointed to rubber-stamp board decisions) tend to be successful people by definition, confident by experience and strong-willed by nature. The number of board members affects the opportunity to make an impression. Too many members and meetings can become protracted. Instead of working towards consensus, divisions may arise and cabals emerge, resulting in adversarial voting. On the other hand, with too few members there may be a shortage of the necessary talents, knowledge and experience.

Maximum and minimum numbers are often prescribed in the company's articles of association and can be amended by the shareholders. Interestingly, a case is often made for increasing the size of the board, seldom for reducing it. Yet as companies evolve situations can arise when a smaller board might be more effective.

In Japan boards of listed companies in *keiretsu* can be very large. (See JAPANESE CORPORATE GOVERNANCE.)

Groups

Major companies these days almost always operate in groups. Sometimes these are relatively simple hierarchies of wholly and partly owned subsidiaries up to a parent company (for example, Marks and Spencer in the UK). In other cases they involve complex networks with hundreds of subsidiary and associated companies.

Directors of companies within such groups can find themselves faced by the problem of "dual lines of control". As directors of the company their duty is to act in the best interests of the shareholders of that company. If the subsidiary is wholly owned by the parent company this may not cause too many problems. If, however, there are minority interests in the company, perhaps a joint-venture partner or a strategic ally, executive directors might find themselves having to choose between what is in the best interests of the company and what is in their interests as executives of the main group. (See REPRESENTATIVE DIRECTOR.)

Board styles

Although the chairman is often called the "chairman of the company", he or she is in reality the chairman of the board. The articles of association of many companies provide for the directors to appoint one of their number to the chair. In other words, the chairman is elected as a director by the shareholders in general meeting, but appointed to the chairmanship by the other directors.

In major companies, however, the role of the chairman has tended to expand to include not only the management of the board meetings (determining the agenda, chairing the meetings and agreeing the minutes), but also a wider responsibility for board matters, such as reviewing board performance and director development. In other cases the chairman takes on a role as a major spokesman for the company, relieving the chief executive officer of such chores.

A long-running debate is whether one person should combine the roles of chief executive and chairman. Those who call for wider conformance from boards say that to split the functions provides necessary checks and balances, and avoids domination by one person. Others point to companies that have been successful because they have been dominated by entrepreneurial figures. They further argue that circumstances can arise when performance issues outweigh conformance issues and tough-minded, single leadership is essential. In Australia and the UK the tendency in major, listed companies is for the roles to be separated, although there are well-known cases of joint roles. In the USA the roles are frequently combined, which has led to criticism from institutional investor organisations that the top executive has too much power. (See DUALITY.)

Board styles

The chairman of the board inevitably has an effect on the way that the board goes about its business. Boards vary enormously. Figure 8 depicts four different board styles, indicating the extent of the directors' concern for their interpersonal relationships at board level, on the one hand, and their tough-minded concern for the work of the board, on the other.

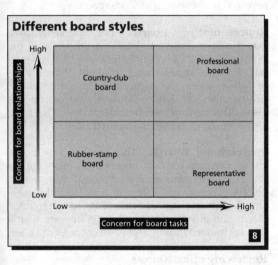

Different board styles

Concern for board relationships

High

Country-club board

Professional board

Rubber-stamp board

Representative board

Low

Low ⟶ High

Concern for board tasks

8

Rubber stamps The directors of a rubber-stamp style board have little concern for either the tasks of the board or the interpersonal relationships between the directors. Examples of such boards can be found in the "letter-box" companies registered in many offshore tax havens. The meetings of the board are a formality. Indeed they are often minuted without them actually taking place. The boards of some closely held private companies also treat their board meetings as a formality; perhaps because one individual is dominant and takes the decisions, or because the key players see each other frequently and decisions are taken in the management context.

Country clubs The country-club board is concerned with interpersonal relations at board level, even if the focus on the issues before the board takes second place. The boards of some old companies, which have been successful in the past, fit this model. There is likely to be a great deal of ritual about board meetings. The boardroom will be beautifully furnished, complete with pictures of previous chairmen. Long-established traditions are revered. Innovation is discouraged.

Representative boards The representative board places more emphasis on the tasks of the board than it does on board relations. It frequently has directors representing different shareholders or stakeholders and is more like a parliament of diverse interests. Issues can easily become politicised. Discussions can be adversarial. The basis and balance of power is important.

Professional boards The professional board shows concern for both the board's tasks and its interpersonal relationships. A board with a successful professional style will have sound leadership from the chair. There will be tough-minded discussion among the members combined with a mutual understanding and respect for each other.

Reviewing effectiveness
There is a danger that the board of a successful company can become complacent and its style of leadership in the boardroom, once so suitable, no longer appropriate. But change is difficult to achieve. There is a need for a strategy for board-level development. The board effectiveness review checklist in Appendix 4 will enable a board's current structure and style to be analysed. Alternatives can be devised, evaluated and discussed in the context of the business strategy. Then a strategy for developing the board and its members can evolve in line with, and as part of, the ongoing strategies to develop the company as a whole.

THE CORPORATE GOVERNANCE DEBATE

The directors' role is integral to the concept of the corporation. Although company law varies from country to country, there are some general points that can usefully be made.

The concept of the company

The original concept of the company was immensely innovative, elegantly simple and proved to be superbly successful. In the middle of the 19th century, apart from companies created by the state or the crown, the only way to do business was as a sole trader or a partnership. If the business became insolvent, the proprietor went to the debtors' prison and his family to the workhouse; hardly an incentive for an investor to risk his funds in a venture run by others. Yet financial incentive was exactly what the businesses growing out of the industrial revolution needed. So the concept of the corporation was created.

In the joint stock, limited liability company the business is incorporated as an independent legal entity, separate from its owners, whose liability for its debts is limited to the amount of equity capital they have agreed to subscribe. A corporate veil is thus drawn round the company, which has many of the rights of a legal person: to buy and sell, to own assets, to incur debts, to employ, to contract and to sue and be sued.

The company has a life of its own. Although this does not guarantee perpetuity, it does give the company an existence independent of the life of the proprietors, who can transfer their shares to others.

Ownership is the basis of power over the company (at least in the Western world): power to nominate and elect the directors, who run the enterprise on behalf of the shareholders; power to require accountability from the directors, the stewards of the business's resources; and power to question them on their report and financial accounts. The members also have independent auditors (in the early days appointed from among themselves) to report that these accounts show a true and fair view of the state of affairs of the company.

The UK adopts company laws
At the beginning of the 19th century to separate a business from its owners would have been thought foolhardy and to restrict the responsibility of owners for their debts immoral. By the end of the century both were commonplace. In 1844 in the UK, the world's leading industrial nation, Parliament passed a Joint Stock Companies Act calling for registration of incorporated companies. In 1855 an act was passed which limited the liability of shareholders. This was followed by a consolidating act in 1862.

British influence in the succeeding years around the world meant that these notions became the basis of company law and corporate governance in many places including the Australian states, the Canadian provinces, Hong Kong, India, New Zealand, Singapore and South Africa. Their company law remains linked through the British Commonwealth, but its extent now varies significantly among jurisdictions. The Companies Act, for example, in Hong Kong runs to less than 400 pages, in Singapore to nearer 600 and in the UK to about 700. At the other extreme, the company law of the British Virgin Islands, a tax haven that has attracted many companies to incorporate because of its undemanding regulatory regime, covers just 100 pages.

The USA follows
Company law developments in the USA evolved along similar lines and reflected similar ideological traditions. Individual states passed legislation to facilitate the incorporation of companies. Governance was again through the meeting of shareholder members in the company. Incorporation of companies at the federal level was not and

is still not available, although federal government does exercise power over securities trading.

Continental Europe goes its own way

Developments in continental Europe followed a different path, reflecting different cultural norms. Companies in Germany, for example, were more heavily regulated and lacked the flexibility of the Anglo-American model. Shareholders' interests are protected by a board of supervision, quite separate from the management of the business. The supervisory board examines and reports on the accounts prepared by the managers. They can call meetings of the shareholders and can, if necessary, change the managers. Top management are thus potentially under greater scrutiny than their Anglo-American counterparts. (But see the Metallgesellschaft case study in Appendix 6. See also TWO-TIER BOARD and GERMAN CORPORATE GOVERNANCE.)

In France the 1807 Napoleonic Code provided the basis for company law. The *société en commandité par actions* was a form of incorporation in which the liability of the managing directors for corporate debts was unlimited while the liability of the outside investors was limited to their equity stake. The *société à responsabilité limitée* was introduced in 1863, giving limited liability to both managing and outside shareholders.

Fundamental differences in company law still survive in Europe, despite the efforts of the European Union's harmonisation programme. The social programme is now being used to impose a degree of regulation, in matters such as worker representation, on companies trading in EU member states.

Anglo-Saxon roots

Thus the original concept of the company is rooted in Anglo-Saxon ideology. The importance attached to the notion of the individual, emphasising personal freedoms and self-regulation under the common law, had a medieval root which contrasted with the more prescriptive rule of law in the continental European jurisdictions which relied on Roman legal traditions.

Different cultures, different opinions

Opinions differ on what the content and boundaries of corporate governance should be. For some the essence is the exercise of power by shareholders; for others it is formal structures of the board and corporate effectiveness that matters; yet others believe the focus should be on the social responsibilities of corporations to a wider set of stakeholders. This book takes the view that corporate governance is concerned with the structure and processes of the board and its relationships with shareholders, regulators, auditors, top management and any other legitimate stakeholders. Figure 9 illustrates the scope of corporate governance in a limited liability company.

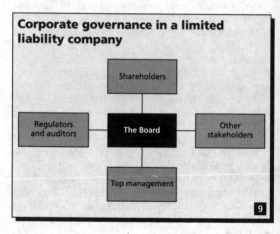

Corporate governance in a limited liability company

Shareholders

Regulators and auditors

The Board

Other stakeholders

Top management

9

Philip Cochran and Steven Wartick, two American scholars writing in 1988, suggested that:

Corporate governance is an umbrella term that includes specific issues arising from interactions among senior management, shareholders, boards of directors, and other corporate stakeholders.

There have been a number of calls for fundamentally rethinking the concept of the corporation. A well-known British management writer, Charles Handy, has recently questioned why ownership was the basis of power in the corporation. "How and why did the concept of property ever enter the debate?" he has asked, offering the alternative of the company as a self-governing, wealth-creating community. But back in 1932 two American researchers, Adolph Berle and Gardiner Means, showed the separation of ownership from control that was occurring, with power concentrated in the hands of management rather than shareholders of large US public companies. Yet most companies' law around the world still assumes a shareholders' democracy as in the 19th century.

Theories of corporate governance

There are five main theories relating to corporate governance.

Stewardship theory Underpinning company law is the requirement that directors show a fiduciary duty towards the shareholders of the company. Inherent in this idea is the belief that the directors can be trusted. Stewardship theory reflects these classical ideas of corporate governance. Power over the corporation is exercised through directors, who are nominated and appointed by the shareholders in general meeting and who are accountable to them for the stewardship over the company's resources, subject to a report to the members from an independent auditor that their accounts show a true and fair view. Stewardship theory remains the theoretical foundation for much regulation and legislation.

Organisation theory was relatively slow to focus on issues at the corporate governance level. In practice, the board of directors was superimposed on few organisation charts; in theory, most organisational studies seemed to assume that organisation structures peaked with the CEO. In recent years, however, there have been some important contributions from the psychology of behavioural and leadership studies and the sociology of organisational and managerial work.

Stakeholder theory emerged during the 1970s, reflecting a fear at the societal level that the large, particularly multinational, corporation had become too large and powerful to be held accountable solely through the classical stewardship mode. Ralph Nader, a passionate advocate of consumer rights in the USA, argued:

> (Giant corporations) can spend decisive amounts to determine which towns thrive and which gather cobwebs, corrupt or help overthrow foreign governments, develop technology that takes lives or saves lives... (The giant corporation) is largely unaccountable to its constituencies – shareholders, workers, consumers, local communities, taxpayers, small businesses, future generations.

In 1975 the Accounting Standards Steering Committee in the UK produced a discussion paper recommending that all economic entities should provide regular accountability reports to all stakeholder groups whose interests might be affected by the decisions of the entity. The political implications of such a heroic idea quickly relegated the report to the files. During the growth and greed era of the 1980s little was heard of stakeholder theories, but in the more environmentally and socially concerned world of the 1990s the ideas are reappearing, for example with socially aware mutual funds.

Agency theory has been a contribution of the 1980s to corporate governance thinking. Although derived from the work of an American economist, Ronald Coarse, in the 1930s, the ideas of agency theory have been applied to directors and boards only in recent years. Inherent in this theoretical perspective is a different view of the nature of man: that he is self-interested rather than altruistic, and that he cannot always be trusted to act in the best interests of others but, rather, to maximise his own utility.

Agency theory presents the relationship between the directors and the shareholders as a contract. Because the directors (the agents) will take decisions in their own interests, the transaction costs of check and balance mechanisms, such as further disclosure, independent outside directors and audit committees of the board, should be incurred to the point at which the reduction of the loss from non-compliance equals the increase in enforcement costs.

Theory of the firm Agency theory and the related transaction-cost economics have become an important component of financial economics and the so-called theory of the firm. A fierce academic debate is still going on between the agency theorists and the stewardship theorists. The former argue that their models are sound and their results statistically revealing: the latter that the same data can be reworked to show opposite effects.

Cultural conundrum

There is, however, another perspective. Stewardship theory, stakeholder theory and agency theory are all essentially ethnocentric. Although the underlying ideological paradigms are seldom articulated, the essential ideas are derived from Western thought, with its perceptions and expectations of the respective roles of individual, enterprise and state and of the relationships between them. But what of other cultures with different perceptions of governance power? (See CHINESE CORPORATE GOVERNANCE and JAPANESE CORPORATE GOVERNANCE.)

Whose company is it anyway?

Implicit in the concept of the joint stock, limited liability company is the belief that ownership provides the basis of power over the corporation. The corporate entity is run for the benefit of the shareholders. Meeting together on a properly convened occasion, the shareholders nominate and elect the directors. Stewardship over the company is exercised by the directors for the benefit of the shareholders. The directors demonstrate their accountability to the shareholders through regular reports and audited financial statements. Such is the conventional wisdom and the legal fiction.

Even in the 19th century it is doubtful if the reality approached this ideal of shareholder democracy, and at the end of the 20th century the unreality is apparent. In the early days of the corporate concept company promoters could, and many did, wield significant power. But at least in those days shareholders were comparatively few and drawn from the ranks of the emerging *rentier* class of the relatively wealthy. They tended to be socially and geographically concentrated. They could actually attend shareholders' meetings.

Today the concept of shareholder democracy has become an anachronism. Individual shareholders are unable to exercise any significant influence, unless they have a sufficient shareholding to be dominant. There are exceptions, of course. In family companies, where owners, directors and managers are often the same people or are closely intertwined, ownership power can be meaningful in influencing board appointments and determining corporate strategies. In subsidiary and associated companies operating in groups or strategic alliance networks, ownership power can be effective, even though control (and power) is often exercised through group organisational control systems not governance mechanisms. Even in public listed companies the power of the proxy vote becomes real should the company be "put into play" through an attempted hostile takeover.

But the conventional wisdom that shareholders determine board membership and can influence corporate direction is, by and large, false; certainly in major public listed companies. Yet commentators continue to call on shareholders to "exercise their power". What power? Commenting on the need to control allegedly excessive director remuneration, the Greenbury Report calls on investors to "use their power and influence" to ensure the implementation of the code of best practice the committee has proposed.

It has been clear for many years, around the commercially advanced world, that individual small shareholders have no real power in governance matters. In the major listed companies shareholdings are widely dispersed and geographically spread. Even with shareholder interest groups and better opportunities to communicate with the other members, individual investors lack the position, prestige or power to influence an incumbent chairman and his or her board.

Institutional muscle

On the other hand, institutional investors do appear to have some power to influence boards, particularly if they act in concert. But this presupposes that the interests of institutional investors are homogeneous, which they are not. The time horizon, risk profile and the interests of the stakeholders of pension funds can be quite different from those of mutual funds and different again from the interests of financial institutions offering private services to wealthy investors. In any case the fund manager voting such shares has already removed the ultimate beneficiary by at least one level from personal shareholder democracy. Moreover, the fund managers of some financial institutions, particularly insurance funds, may have difficulty in voting the shares of some of their holdings.

Certainly institutional investor pressure, such as that exerted by Pension Investment Research Consultants (PIRC) in the UK and Calpers (the Californian State Employees pension fund) in the USA, has been influential in sharpening up boardroom attitudes. The removal of the chairmen and boards of under-performing companies in recent years, including American Express, IBM and General Motors, makes the point. But such institutional pressure has not (at least in the short term) always benefited the shareholders. In the case of Saatchi & Saatchi, the removal of the dominant entrepreneur resulted in him setting up a competing firm, taking significant accounts with him, and a decline in the share price of the original firm (renamed Cordiant) that the shareholder action was supposed to address (see Appendix 6).

Relationship investing, in which the institutional investor takes a major stake and a long-term interest in return for a seat on the board and therefore a chance to influence board decisions, might be seen to offer a greater chance of shareholder influence. But again there is no guarantee that what is good for investors such as Warren Buffett or Robert Monks is consistent with the goals of the other shareholders. Relationship investing is not a return to shareholder democracy.

In fairness, the attempts by the boards of some major firms to communicate with their shareholders should be acknowledged. Shareholder meetings in various locations, an array of publications, videos of annual meetings, invitations to meet and question the directors: these are all attempts to inform those with an interest in the company. But it should be remembered that they are also intended to maintain shareholder support and to influence share prices positively, a valuable operation if raising new funds – and for those who have executive share options they want to exercise.

Time for change

It is clear that the 19th century concept of the corporation, based on ownership power, has become inadequate. But as we approach the 21st century other problems have arisen. Modern settlement systems leave the investments of small shareholders in nominee companies. How are these shares to be voted? Huge sums of money are also being invested in warrants and other forms of derivative instruments, so the ultimate owners are yet further removed from voting power over the corporate entities in which the investments are based. Who is now to exercise power over companies?

The way ahead

Perhaps the way ahead is to face up to the reality. Shareholders can, at best, influence corporate behaviour: they can no longer wield overall governance power. Power lies with the incumbent board. The ultimate power is the right to nominate and appoint to that board.

So the crucial question becomes: who should wield the power to appoint directors, and by what mechanisms? A nominating committee made up of independent outside directors is the current preferred response. But even if nominating committees of independent non-executive directors are created, might they not reflect the interests of the board incumbents, who nominated them and with whom they have to work, rather than the interests of the shareholders?

Creating a nominating committee begs the question: who chooses the outside directors on the nominating committee? Might they not form a cosy club of like-minded executives from other companies, perhaps with cross-directorships? As Juvenal, a Roman satirist and poet, said: "*quis custodiet ipsos custodes?*" (Who will guard the guards?) But then he was worried about those he had set to guard his wife as he went off to war. A shareholder committee, perhaps? But how to produce a slate of genuine alternatives? Candidate manifestos? Now we are back to the stakeholder arguments of the 1970s. A separate shareholder supervisory committee? A two-tier board?

It is very unlikely that an ideal solution exists, but the next few years are likely to produce some revolutionary new thinking on the role of boards and the work of their directors. Nothing less than a complete reinvention of the 19th century, Western concept of the corporation is likely to suffice: one that does not merely treat companies as either private or public, but that can reflect the reality of governance power in complex group chains and networks, strategic alliances and cross-held corporate entities.

CONFLICTS FACING DIRECTORS

Corporate governance is about the exercise of power over corporate entities. At the beginning of the 1980s the term corporate governance was seldom used; today it is commonplace. Around the world issues of corporate governance are exciting the interest of academics and professionals alike; even the popular press carries commentaries on the subject. In the USA, the removal of dominant chief executives has been brought about by pressure from institutional investors, dissatisfied with their companies' strategic direction. Relationship investing suggests closer links between institutional shareholders and management. In the UK, the Cadbury Report of the Committee on the Financial Aspects of Corporate Governance (1992) and the Greenbury Report on Directors' Remuneration (1995) have created codes of conduct for public companies on governance matters. Around the world accountability for allegedly excessive director remuneration has become a concern. Nor are the issues of governance limited to the public company. Privatisation and corporatisation of entities previously in the public domain have added a new set of issues. World recession on the one hand and top management succession on the other have given many family firms their share of governance problems. In the modern world, even the non-profit sector – universities, cultural societies, professional institutions, for example – seems to have its share of problems at the level of the governing body.

Company law and regulation

The body of company law in the jurisdiction in which the company is incorporated, and sometimes where it does business, determines many of the responsibilities faced by directors in that state or country. Further duties may arise from the laws of insolvency, consumer protection, monopoly and merger control, employment, environmental protection and so on. For the director of a public company, whose shares are traded on a stock exchange, the laws of securities trading and investor protection also apply, as well as the rules of the specific stock exchange itself.

Trends
Two trends are affecting directors' legal responsibilities.

1 Legislators around the world are tending to increase the statutory requirements regulating companies and requiring disclosure of corporate affairs. Moreover, there are forces encouraging the convergence of regulation.

Securities regulation and corporate governance rules over the world's listed companies are converging under the auspices of the International Organisation of Securities Commissions (IOSCO), whose membership includes most of the world's securities regulatory bodies, from the Securities and Exchange Commission in the USA to the Securities and Futures Commission in Hong Kong. IOSCO members have agreed to exchange information on unusual trades, thus making global insider trading easier to detect.

The International Accounting Standards Committee and the International Auditing Practices Committee of the International Federation of Accountants also have close links with the IOSCO and are further forces working towards international harmonisation and standardisation of financial reporting and auditing practices.

2 Shareholders and other parties feeling aggrieved about the way the directors have been running companies have increasingly been resorting to litigation. The lead came from the USA, where the contingent fee system (whereby lawyers are paid a percentage of whatever damages are awarded or agreed) and class actions (that is the possibility of joining all the members of a specific class, such as shareholders, in a claim without their specific consent) is widely believed to have encouraged litigation. But other countries, including Australia, Canada and the UK, have also seen an increase in actions brought against companies, boards, individual directors and the companies' auditors.

Insurance cover for negligence or other claims against directors and other company officials has proved increasingly necessary and premiums have risen accordingly. Indeed, there are a growing number of cases in which prominent people have refused directorships because of the exposure, not only to the threat of litigation and financial costs, but also to the media interest and personal approbation that can follow a legal action, even if successfully defended.

Directors' remuneration

If the corporate governance *cri de coeur* of the 1980s was occasioned by the excesses of predators and the paraphernalia of poison pills, greenmail, white knights and the rest, the emerging clamour of the 1990s is about allegedly excessive board-level remuneration and the associated rolling contracts, share options and golden handshakes. "Put the brakes on the gravy train" thundered *The Times* in 1994. In the UK the media has led the debate, but institutional investors have also been challenging board-level compensation.

Pay On the level of directors' remuneration, the National Institute for Economic and Social Research (NIESR) has shown that directors' pay in the UK rose (in the 169 companies surveyed) by 77% in real terms between 1985 and 1990, while average earnings in these companies rose by only 17%. The institute found a clear relationship between board-level pay and sales growth but only a weak one with returns to investors. Directors' pay grew faster in firms which had grown by acquisition, it found, than in those which had relied on internal plough-back of profits. But the NIESR report has been attacked for failing to take the effects of share options into account.

Payoffs The effect of rolling contracts for directors, of course, is to boost the payoff for directors whose contracts are terminated (or who follow the face-saving formula of "retiring" by agreement). The Cadbury Committee recommended that two years should be the maximum period for such contracts, although three years remains quite normal. The shareholders of a number of major companies have been challenging the rolling three-year contracts enjoyed by their directors. The National Association of Pension Funds, having sought the views of its members, seems to think that rolling contracts should be limited to no more than one year and any fixed-term contracts should not be for more than three years.

The scale of golden handshakes has certainly been rising in the UK. In 1994 *The Independent* newspaper cited two pay-outs of over £3m, four over £2m and six over £1m. Moreover, there have been some cases of top executives, who have proven to be incompetent, being well rewarded for their failure. Five directors of Tiphook, a container and trailer rental firm, received some £6m between them, following a board reshuffle after the company reported a £330m loss.

Share options On the matter of share options, the intention is inherently sound: to reward good performance by linking director remuneration to improvements in the share price. Unfortunately there are major drawbacks. For one thing, share option schemes tend to reward general rises in the market that are unrelated to the performance of the company itself; for another, poor performance that pulls the share price down carries no penalty.

Privatised particulars In the UK privatised utilities have come in for particular criticism. In many cases with near monopoly markets, top management have become millionaires, not because they built up the business through their entrepreneurial flair, nor because of personal risk or any special contribution to performance, but because they happened to be in the right place at the right time. High salaries, generous share options and contract termination provisions have all been criticised.

The going rate

Arguments advanced to support relatively high remuneration levels are the need to attract the best people and to retain existing directors. Sir Robert Clarke, chairman of Thames Water, justifying three-year contracts, explained that they were necessary "to attract the right people" and that "it would be unfair not to extend the same benefit to existing directors". Comparisons with levels of reward in other countries is also often cited in justification. Other arguments include the need for comparability with similar companies and with the professions (such as the lawyers and auditors to the company), and to maintain differentials with non-board senior executive staff. Comparability with the rewards of stars of the sporting and entertainment worlds is less easy to sustain; but comparisons with top military personnel, and the staff of the United Nations, World Bank and European Union can provide some indicators.

Towards a solution

There are three potential levels of control.

Self-control at the board level This is crucial, and includes the influence of independent non-executive directors, particularly those who serve on the remuneration committee of the board, if there is one. But since so many outside directors are themselves top executives and directors of other companies, the fear of mutual back-scratching is always present. The Cadbury Committee emphasised the importance of non-executive directors and, like the subsequent Greenbury Report, recommended remuneration committees, requiring listed companies to state whether they had one and to explain the formula by which they worked. Most companies appear to have established a remuneration committee, but few say how they work. The separation of the CEO role from that of the board chairman could also provide a counter to remuneration policies dominated by the CEO; an idea that could be particularly pertinent in the USA.

Influence at shareholder level Shareholders are hampered by having to rely on the information they are given in, for example, the directors' report and the audited accounts. The absence of details of directors' contracts makes argument difficult, particularly in general meetings that are dominated by a chairman with proxy votes to hand. A stronger potential lies with the institutional investors, although a spokesman for the National Association of Pension Funds in the UK has pointed out that "the sums involved (in directors' remuneration) are often 'flea-bites' as far as the earnings of most big companies are concerned ... fund managers are interested in share price and profits performance not what directors pay themselves". Relationship investing in which institutional investors take a significant, long-term stake in a company could be more influential.

Control at the societal level Social disapproval, often expressed through the media, can affect attitudes. Tim Melville-Ross, director-general of the influential Institute of Directors in London, has said: "I am perfectly happy about the idea of real entrepreneurs who take big risks taking away substantial rewards. But for bureaucrats to be similarly rewarded is wrong." Stock market regulators or fund managers might develop exhortatory guidelines. As a matter of political judgment, governments could introduce tax disincentives or even legal sanctions and mandatory limits.

What's right?

The real issue is not so much how to design mechanisms that regulate and control directors' remuneration, but how to determine the "right" amount that will reward contribution and risk, and will control greed and avoid envy. In other words, to decide what is fair and reasonable and is seen to be so. Bill Gates, CEO of Microsoft, one of the most successful companies in the USA, is one of the lowest-paid CEOs in corporate America. His salary and bonus in 1992 totalled $285,000. Of course his holding in the company he created makes him one of the richest men in the USA. In the same year the chairman of much less successful IBM had a base salary of $2m, plus a bonus of $5m for leaving his previous job and stock options that would be worth $50m if he could get IBM's stock price back to 1986 levels. What are needed now are some benchmarks that relate reward to long-term performance.

New complexities

A final area of conflict in corporate governance arises as a result of the complexity of structures now being adopted in international business. Single corporate entities are a thing of the past, except in small and family firms. Instead we find complex networks of subsidiary and associated companies, cross-holdings, public companies with chained ownership giving leveraged power to those at the top, private companies and limited partnerships controlling public listed companies, and many other forms of strategic alliances which have changed the power relationship from that envisaged in the original corporate concept.

Power base

The essence of governance is power. A British Labour prime minister, Harold Wilson, in his book *The Governance of Britain,* wrote of the power to govern at the level of the state. Corporate governance is the exercise of power at the level of the corporate entity. In the 19th century, when the brilliantly innovative concept of the joint stock limited liability company was conceived, ownership was the undisputed basis of power. So it still is in most jurisdictions according to company law. But how different is the reality.

Today power over a corporation can lie with several, often competing, groups of people. Institutional investors have rediscovered the ability to influence corporate affairs, particularly in the USA where the former chairmen of some major corporations rue the institutions' new-found powers. Relationship investors aim to wield power through a significant and long-term commitment to the corporation. In Germany power on the supervisory board is shared between labour and capital. In the Netherlands it is a tripartite relationship between capital, labour and the public interest. France permits a number of alternative power bases. In Japan the powers behind the *keiretsu* wield the power. In China the state still seeks to exercise an influence over corporate entities.

Cadbury stirred it up...

The Cadbury report on corporate governance provoked a wide range of reactions. On the one hand there were those who complained that the report failed to go far enough to tackle the perceived problems of the abuse of power in listed companies, particularly those dominated by strong chairmen and CEOs. The report lacked teeth, it was argued. The code was voluntary, lacking legislative sanctions, with the ultimate threat of delisting from the stock exchange likely to harm shareholders, the very people Cadbury was supposed to be protecting. On the other hand, there was a vehement lobby which believed that the proposals – for the separation of chairman from CEO, powerful audit committees and independent directors with their own leader if necessary – were an attack on the very notion of the unitary board, introducing the suspect continental European two-tier board by the back door.

...and brought about changes

Given these two dramatically contrasting views, Cadbury probably got it about right: certainly for starters. The significant effects that the report has had in the UK are only now becoming clear, including changed attitudes towards board-level professionalism, wider disclosure on governance matters and in the continuing debate on governance issues.

The effect has been felt beyond the UK. In Canada, Singapore, South Africa and other Commonwealth countries issues raised by Cadbury have been debated. In Australia Cadbury was influential in prompting a major reappraisal of governance, culminating in the Hilmer Report which took a different line from Cadbury. It argued that, although concern with shareholder protection was an important part of the board's duty, its key role was to ensure that corporate management was continuously and effectively striving for above-average performance, taking account of risk. In Hong Kong a direct result was a new requirement that all listed companies should have two independent non-executive directors. This may not appear dramatic, but it will change the balance of governance power, given that the Hong Kong Stock Exchange board has only one company that is truly in the hands of the public; the remainder are controlled to greater or lesser extent by dominant owners, particularly overseas Chinese family-based firms.

Adapting for the future

Corporate governance entails far more than financial control. It is about the exercise of power over the most influential entities in modern society. Future developments of corporate governance need to go way beyond discussions of board structures and governance mechanisms to focus on the reality of corporate power. What really happens at board level? What should happen? How is strategy formulated? Should the board set the corporate direction? Who supervises executive performance? To whom is the company and its board accountable? To whom should it be? The exercise of power (governance) over companies in the 21st century will depend on the answers to these questions.

Part 2

A–Z

A SHARE

See DIFFERENT TYPES OF SHARES.

ACCOUNTABILITY

The directors of a company are primarily account-able to the shareholders. Such accountability is normally achieved through the regular DIRECTORS' REPORT AND ACCOUNTS and the ANNUAL GENERAL MEET-ING of the members (that is of the EQUITY share-holders) of the company. In most jurisdictions, however, there has been a tendency to call for wider accountability from boards, particularly in a PUBLIC COMPANY. Regulators demand wider disclo-sure of financial and other information. Employ-ees' representatives expect information on matters that could affect their interests. (In Germany, the Netherlands and Sweden employees have statu-tory rights to board-level accountability.) Cus-tomer and other interest groups call for greater transparency of company activities. STAKEHOLDER THEORY argues that public companies have a duty to be accountable to all interest groups which could be affected by the company's actions (including customers, distributors, employees, financial institutions and suppliers, as well as local, national and international public interests).

> *The directors of companies, being managers rather of other people's money than their own, it cannot well be expected that they should watch over it with the same anxious vigilance with which the partners in a private copartnery frequently watch over their own*
> Adam Smith, *Wealth of Nations*, 1776

ADDED-VALUE CHAIN ANALYSIS

Every business exists within the added-value chain within its industry; for example, the farmer grows wheat, the miller turns it into flour, the transport company carries it to the baker where it is baked, or to the supermarket where it is sold to the end-user. Similarly each company has an added-value chain as the product or service is prepared for delivery to the customer.

A business may be heavily integrated with an upstream supply division or downstream channels; or at the other end of the scale it might have outsourced all but a core competence. The shoe firm Reebok, for example, has hardly any manufacturing and no retailing outlets, just a highly profitable managerial and marketing function. Analysing the elements of the added-value chain in a business can provide valuable strategic insights. Figure 10 illustrates a value-chain analysis for an electricity supply company.

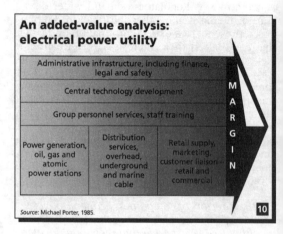

An added-value analysis: electrical power utility

Administrative infrastructure, including finance, legal and safety			M A R G I N
Central technology development			
Group personnel services, staff training			
Power generation, oil, gas and atomic power stations	Distribution services, overhead, underground and marine cable	Retail supply, marketing, customer liaison – retail and commercial	

Source: Michael Porter, 1985.

Each of the boxes in Figure 10 can be exploded into a whole set or hierarchy of more detailed diagrams that show just where value is being added. If associated with the related costs, a value-chain analysis will highlight which elements are driving costs and which are adding value. This information can be very important in STRATEGY FORMULATION because it can pinpoint the CORE COMPETENCES of the company and show how its activities are differentiated from those of alternative sources of supply. It can suggest new strategic options – both for improving existing activities and for developing new strategies such as outsourcing, backwards or forwards integration by acquisition, mergers or strategic alliances with firms offering similar services to obtain scale economies – share risk and enhance development.

ADJOURNMENT OF MEETINGS
See MEETING MANIPULATION.

ADVISORY BOARD
A non-statutory committee, typically without executive power, formed in various parts of the world by companies operating internationally, to give advice to the corporate directors and other decision-makers. Prominent business leaders, politicians and other influential figures from that region are usually invited to serve. Advisory boards were more prevalent in the 1970s and early 1980s. Companies have since found that the advice they need can be obtained more cheaply from consultants and commentators who can be retained only for as long as their advice is required. Some also found that advisory boards, although they had no formal executive authority, could create complications by making policy recommendations that were inconsistent with group-wide needs. For example, the advisory board might recommend investment in a given country, when the board's global strategy called for disinvestment there.

---

*Isn't it time we promoted young George
to the board?
But Mr George is 62.
Is he really? How well I remember his father.*

AGE OF DIRECTORS
An OUTSIDE DIRECTOR or NON-EXECUTIVE DIRECTOR tends to be older than an EXECUTIVE DIRECTOR. Three factors can restrict the age of directors: company law, which typically requires directors to be under 70 unless the shareholders have duly approved an exception; the company's own ARTICLES OF ASSOCIATION; and, for listed companies, the LISTING RULES of the relevant stock exchange.

A

AGENCY THEORY

A statistically powerful, theoretical base that can be used for gaining insights into the effect of a company's board on the performance of the business. The theory, as described by Jensen and Meckling in the *Journal of Financial Economics* in 1976, sees the relationship between directors and shareholders as:

> *A contract under which one or more persons (the principals) engage another person (the agent) to perform some service on their behalf which includes delegating some decision-making authority to the agent. If both parties to the relationship are utility maximisers there is good reason to believe the agent will not always act in the best interests of the principal.*

Exponents of agency theory quote examples of directors who have failed to act in the interests of the shareholders, treating the company as though it was their private fiefdom. Much research, using agency theory methods, has been published on board-level activities. Frequently these studies have attempted to show relationships between aspects of governance, such as board structure, DUALITY or directors' rewards, and overall corporate performance. But much of this work has been based on published data, such as the annual financial performance and board structures, and, furthermore, it has often been done by young researchers who have never met a company director.

As with some other powerful theories, agency theory provides a wonderfully (over) simple explanation of an aspect of economic life. Reality, unfortunately, is more complicated. Board behaviour does not consist exclusively of individual contractual relationships, but is influenced by interpersonal behaviour, group dynamics and political intrigue. Nor do all directors act in a way that makes the most of their personal interests: they can act responsibly with independence and integrity, as envisaged by the alternative STEWARD-

SHIP THEORY. Nevertheless, insights from the research can challenge the shibboleths of conventional wisdom about the way boards work.

Statistical methods will not explain the reality of the boardroom.

Ada Demb at the Strategic Management Society Conference, 1993

AGENDA

The order in which items are to be covered in a meeting. There are three approaches to agenda design.

1 The routine approach, in which each meeting follows the pattern of the previous one: apologies, approval of the MINUTES, matters arising, the usual substantive items and any other business.

2 The chairman-led approach, in which the chairman determines the agenda. Sir Norman Chester, who became warden of Nuffield College, Oxford, after a career in the British civil service, believed that good chairmen, among which he counted himself, should put much effort into designing agenda. He recommended that care should be taken in selecting the items to be discussed, the time that should be allocated to each and their positioning on the agenda. Matters likely to be controversial should come towards the end, when members were expecting the meeting to end or had already left, thus increasing the chairman's chances of getting the decision he wants. He also believed in drafting the minutes along with the agenda, because those who draft the minutes – as every ambitious civil servant knows – can make them reflect their point of view.

3 The professional chairman approach, in which the chairman seeks advice on the agenda, perhaps from the COMPANY SECRETARY, or by asking each director whether there are items they wish to see discussed. Lord Caldecote, when chairman of the Delta Group, wrote to each of his directors periodically to ask whether there were matters they felt that the board should be discussing for the future benefit of the firm.

AGM
See ANNUAL GENERAL MEETING.

ALLIANCE BUILDING
See GAMES DIRECTORS PLAY.

ALTERNATE DIRECTOR
The ARTICLES OF ASSOCIATION of some companies allow the board to nominate alternate directors. This can be useful if board members have to travel a lot or are based out of the country in which board meetings are usually held. When serving in the alternate capacity, the alternate director has all the rights to INFORMATION and all the duties and responsibilities of every other director.

ANNUAL GENERAL MEETING
A properly convened meeting of all the voting EQUITY shareholders of the company. The annual general meeting (AGM) is part of the formal machinery of CORPORATE GOVERNANCE, providing an opportunity for the directors to demonstrate their ACCOUNTABILITY to the owners. Certain decisions, such as the approval of the annual accounts and dividend, the appointment of directors and the confirmation of the auditors, are statutorily required to be taken by the AGM. The detailed rules, such as the amount of notice required and rules for voting (including proxy votes), are usually contained in the company's ARTICLES OF ASSOCIATION. Some jurisdictions allow small, closely held companies to forgo their AGM, because all members can be presumed to know the company's affairs sufficiently well and to be able to exert their influence over them.

In the USA directors of listed companies expect to be extensively questioned at their AGMs. Indeed, they are often briefed, even rehearsed, on possible enquiries. In Japan the AGMs of all listed companies are nearly always held on the same day to prevent the disruption of the meeting by paid troublemakers from the YAKUZA. In the UK and most European countries, by contrast, AGMS have tended to be brief, formal, entirely predictable affairs in which any sign of critical questioning is thwarted from the chair and the only shareholder comment is a vote of thanks to the chairman and the board. Recently, however, there have been signs of an end to that complacency. Institutional and private investors have begun to demand answers to questions on matters such as DIRECTORS' REMUNERATION and the company's (and by implication its board's) performance.

AMAKADURI
See DESCENT FROM HEAVEN.

ARTICLES OF ASSOCIATION
The formal set of rules by which a company is run. Registered with the company regulatory authorities at the time of incorporation, in accordance with the company law in that jurisdiction, the articles provide an important element in the CORPORATE GOVERNANCE mechanisms. Articles can be amended by a resolution formally approved by a meeting of the company's members. Directors should always study the articles of a company on whose board they serve. Occasionally non-standard drafting can have unexpected effects on director powers and board decisions. For example, an owner-manager of a company incorporated in the UK that was in a joint venture with a Japanese SHAREHOLDER was thwarted in his attempt to bring in new capital. He believed he had control because he held 61% of the voting shares, only to discover that to exercise such powers, the articles called for the approval of 75% of the shareholders.

ASSOCIATE DIRECTOR
Some companies give the title of director to senior managers, even though they are not formally on the board. One reason might be to reward managerial performance with recognition and status; another might be to give prestige to an executive

who is required to represent the company with clients, customers or government. Sometimes such employees are called associate directors. Even though they have not been appointed by the shareholders, nor recognised as directors by the filing requirements of companies' acts and stock exchange listing agreements, such people could find themselves held responsible like other directors if those with whom they had dealt reasonably thought they were directors. (See also TITLES.)

AUDIT

In most jurisdictions companies are required to have an audit so that the auditors can report to the shareholders that the annual report and accounts presented to them by the directors show a true and fair view of the state of the company's affairs, although the exact wording varies. In some jurisdictions quarterly accounts also have to be audited; in others closely held private companies may dispense with the audit, if the shareholders agree; and in a few, such as the British Virgin Islands, there is no audit requirement at all.

AUDIT COMMITTEE

The relationship with the external, independent auditors is crucial to board-level effectiveness. All directors need to know what issues have arisen during the AUDIT. The board must avoid the possibility of a powerful executive director, such as the finance director or the CEO, dominating the relationship with the AUDITOR, resolving all matters before they reach the board. An audit committee can avoid such problems. A subcommittee of the main board, the audit committee is made up wholly, or with a majority, of outside directors. Its role is to act as a bridge between the external auditors and the board. Typically audit committees meet three or four times a year to discuss the details of the audit, to consider any contentious points that have arisen in the accounts and to receive the auditor's recommendations on audit matters such as management controls.

The audit committee will also usually be concerned with the appointment of auditors and the negotiation of the audit fee. Problems can arise if an audit committee goes beyond its bridging role with the auditors and begins to interfere in management's legitimate responsibilities. The New York Stock Exchange requires an audit committee as a condition of listing. In the UK the Cadbury Committee on the financial aspects of CORPORATE GOVERNANCE strongly recommended an audit committee in its code of best practice.

AUDITOR

Independent outside auditors fulfil a crucial role in CORPORATE GOVERNANCE. Usually appointed formally by the members, on the recommendation of the incumbent board, the auditors report on the directors' report and accounts submitted to the members by the board. Should the AUDIT throw up disagreements that cannot be reconciled with the company's directors, the auditor will qualify the audit report. In recent years auditors of major public companies around the world have found themselves the subject of LITIGATION from dissatisfied shareholders and others when subsequent events raise questions about the validity of audited financial statements. This can be caused by the DEEP POCKET SYNDROME. To ensure that the findings of the auditors are available to the entire board, including any outside directors, conventional wisdom now recommends the creation of an AUDIT COMMITTEE.

AUFSICHTSRAT

The upper SUPERVISORY BOARD of the German form of TWO-TIER BOARD. Large companies in Germany are seen as a form of "partnership" between capital and labour. Reflecting this approach to worker co-determination, the *Aufsichtsrat* has half its members representing the shareholders and half the employees. (See also the Metallgesellschaft case study in Appendix 6.)

B SHARE

Each EQUITY share normally carries one vote; indeed "one share, one vote" has been a cause pursued by some advocates of SHAREHOLDER democracy. Occasionally, however, dominant owner-managers in public companies find the need for additional funding from the public, but realise that issuing more shares will dilute their holdings below the point at which they can maintain control. A way round this is to issue some B shares carrying a disproportionately large number of votes (perhaps 100) per share. In this way the additional equity shares will not dilute their voting capacity below the controlling level.

A good example of the use of B shares is the activities of the late Dr An Wang, who built up Wang Laboratories dramatically during the 1970s and early 1980s. Though highly successful at that time, ploughing back profits was not enough to fund the additional capital needs of the rapidly expanding company. But raising more capital on the market would have diluted the voting power of the shares owned by the founder below that needed to maintain control. Like other Chinese entrepreneurs, Dr Wang wanted to keep control within the family. Wang Laboratories was listed on the New York Stock Exchange, which at that time did not allow the DUAL CLASS SHARE. So Dr Wang re-listed the shares on the smaller American Stock Exchange. He was advised that the share price might suffer because investors would view the shares as more risky, with the company dominated by him and his family interests. In the event the share price increased following the re-listing with B shares. For a while the company continued to prosper, but it eventually failed to adapt to strategic changes in its markets and family control was lost.

BOARD EFFECTIVENESS

There was a time when a director had to do little more than attend an occasional meeting, make a few personal observations and look forward to receiving a fee. But that was in the days when people rode to meetings on a horse. Today shareholders, regulators and other stakeholders have high expectations of directors. Requirements from regulators continue to grow, pressures from institutional investors have become significant, and there is an increasing threat of LITIGATION against the company, the board and individual directors for malpractice or negligence. Under such circumstances the need for board-level effectiveness has never been higher. In response some boards are now specifically considering the CORE COMPETENCES that are needed in directors, systematically reviewing the performance of the board, and developing strategies for board-level development.

Outside directors never know enough about the business to be useful and inside directors always know too much to be independent.

BOARD GUIDELINES

Few companies, including even the most significant around the world, have written board guidelines. General Motors is one exception. Its seemingly exhaustive guidelines for the board (see Appendix 3) include guidance on:

- the separation of chairman and CEO;
- the concept of LEAD DIRECTOR;
- the number of board committees;
- the assignment and rotation of committee members;
- the frequency and length of committee meetings;
- committee AGENDA;
- the selection of agenda items for board meetings;
- board materials distributed in advance;
- presentations to the directors;
- regular attendance of non-directors at board meetings;
- executive sessions of outside directors;
- board access to senior management;
- board compensation review;

- size of the board;
- mix of inside and outside directors;
- definition of independence for outside directors;
- former CEO's board membership;
- board membership criteria;
- selection of new directors;
- assessing the board's performance;
- directors who change their present job responsibilities;
- term limits;
- retirement age;
- evaluation of the CEO;
- board succession planning;
- top management development;
- board interaction with institutional investors, the press, customers and other stakeholders.

More companies could usefully follow suit.

BOARD LIFE CYCLE

Businesses have a tendency to outgrow their boards. A successful contribution to the board in the past does not guarantee a continuing contribution in the future, if the strategic situation facing the company changes significantly. Yet few boards have formal director development and succession plans; even fewer have a strategy for board development that will ensure that the board changes in line with proposed changes in the overall corporate strategy.

The most important factor governing a successful board is the quality of the board itself ... Board meetings must not be solemn affairs ... There is no absolute magic formula. Every company has its own culture and metabolism, and different types of business require separate types of management style and approach from the board.
Sir Richard Greenbury, chairman of Marks and Spencer, UK

BOARD MEETING

A board of directors can meet when and where it

wants, subject to anything in the ARTICLES OF ASSO-CIATION. Some boards have few meetings, either because the directors tend to meet regularly on an informal basis, so that the board meetings become an occasion for formalising decisions taken, or because the activities of the company do not require more meetings. Professional boards, however, usually have a regular schedule of meetings (often monthly). (See also BOARD STYLE.)

The Board of IBM in the late 1980s was far too large, with 18 members, to be an effective committee. It was headed by a chairman who was also the chief executive; it was stuffed with retirees (a third of the number, including the former chairman); and it was short on relevant business experience. Eight members were drafted from other industries. None of their companies manufactured or marketed in ways remotely analogous to IBM's processes and procedures and needs. The others included a lawyer, three academics and the former secretary for defence. Few held any significant ownership stake in IBM. This type of boardroom construction works well for a company that is running well and is led by an executive team which knows where it is going and why. In cases like IBM during the crisis years, more was required of the outside directors than they could provide in terms of relevant and current business experience and skills.

Wong Kai Wa, Aaron: the perspective of an MBA student

BOARD STRUCTURE

The UNITARY BOARD has both executive and outside non-executive directors. In many small and family firms the board is entirely executive; others have a minority non-executive membership. Yet others, including the majority of public companies in Australia and the USA, have a majority of outside directors. A few companies, particularly in the non-profit sector, have an entirely non-executive board, with the chief executive and possibly other top executives in attendance. The minimum and maximum size of a board may be constrained by the ARTICLES OF ASSOCIATION, which may be amended with the formal approval of the shareholders.

> *Board dynamics concern the influences acting on the boundaries of board structure. Boards are relatively transient and often in unstable condition.*
> Robert Kirk Mueller, *Board Score*, 1982

> *Boards should play greater attention to the calibre as well as the mix of directors, recognising that effective board membership requires high levels of intellectual ability, experience, soundness of judgment and integrity.*
> The Hilmer Report, *Strictly Boardroom*, Australia 1993

BOARD STYLE

Boards can vary dramatically in their approach to their work. Some have a rather comfortable, club-like style, others tend to act as a rubber stamp for management proposals. Some have directors who represent various interest groups and are consequently more political in style, while others adopt a professional approach with a concern for both the strategic direction of the company and the supervision of executive performance.

> *What matters is not only the structure of boards but how they work.*
> Sir Adrian Cadbury, speaking in Australia, 1993

> *... there was no attempt to make management accountable to anyone. On the contrary boards of directors – legally the governing body of the corporation – became increasingly impotent rubber stamps for a company's top management.*
> Peter Drucker, *Post-capitalist Society*, 1993

> *To my way of thinking the General Motors board has a unique function of great significance. That is what I call an "audit function". I do not mean*

*audit in the usual financial sense but one that
contemplates a continuous review and appraisal
of what is going on throughout the enterprise.
It is impossible to conceive of every member of
the corporation's board of directors having
intimate knowledge of, and business experience
in, every one of the technical matters which
require top level consideration or action.
Nevertheless, the board can and should be
responsible for the end result.*

Alfred P. Sloan, *My Years with General Motors*, 1963

*The words of Mr Sloan take on a new
significance: "I happen to be one of the old school
who thinks that a knowledge of the business is
essential to a successful organisation." That is
simply not the case today at General Motors.*

John de Lorean, *On a Clear Day You Can See General Motors*,
1979

(Of course this was long before General Motors introduced
the Board Guidelines that are reproduced in Appendix 3.)

BOESKY, IVAN

A securities dealer in the USA who epitomised the
money and growth culture of the 1980s. A col-
league of Dennis LEVINE, Ivan Boesky told a business school graduation ceremony at the University
of California: "I want you to know that I think that
greed is healthy. It is the basis of the capitalist system." He received rapturous applause; such was
the business climate in the mid-1980s. Subsequently, he went to jail on INSIDER DEALING charges.

BUDGETARY PLANNING

An approach to STRATEGY FORMULATION. If
entrepreneurial strategies developed by the
founder of a business seem to be failing, the other
directors may try to superimpose order. Often
they call for more formal planning, more control
of acquisitions and investment decisions and less
reactive deal-making. Budgetary planning and
control is emphasised, so that the board can
approve spending plans and be more closely

involved in monitoring performance. More man
agers within the organisation now participate in
the planning process, forecasting anticipated lev
els of activity, planned revenues, costs and profits
Such planning is often tied to formal accounting
processes and annual budgets and is financially
oriented, relatively short-term and based on inter
nal organisational units such as cost and profit
centres.

Critics of accountancy-based planning systems
argue that they cannot be truly strategic because
they are short-term, linked to annual accounting
cycles and do not reflect the natural strategic time
horizons of the business. Proponents of finan-
cially-based planning suggest that this problem
can be overcome by long-range planning, in
which forecasts are projected further forward and
budget plans extended for longer periods, perhaps three to five years. If competition and markets were relatively predictable and slow to
change, this might be feasible. In most of today's
globally influenced markets it is not.

Two other criticisms of financially oriented
corporate planning are that it undervalues other
vital factors, such as product and market strategies, and it is company centred. The strategist is
inside the company looking out, whereas HELI-
COPTER VISION is needed, that is looking down at
the company in its industry and market context.

BULLOCK REPORT

Sir Alan Bullock (now Lord Bullock), when master
of St Catherine's College, Oxford, was asked in
1976 by the British prime minister, Harold Wilson
(leader of the Labour Party), to chair an inquiry
into industrial democracy. This was a response to
the European Community's proposals, in the fifth
draft directive on company law harmonisation,
that major companies in all EC countries should
adopt the German TWO-TIER BOARD structure in
which half the members of the SUPERVISORY BOARD
represented capital (elected by the shareholders)
and the other half represented employees (elected
through trade union representation). The Bullock

Report recommended the continuation of the British type of UNITARY BOARD, but it did suggest that a proportion of the directors be elected, through trade union machinery, to represent employee concerns. Business interests were highly critical of the proposals and the draft fifth directive has never been enacted.

CADBURY REPORT

Prominent institutions in the City of London, concerned about AUDIT and regulatory issues following a number of dramatic company collapses in the 1980s, set up a committee chaired by Sir Adrian Cadbury. To avoid the potential domination of companies by over-powerful chief executives or over-enthusiastic executive management, the committee's 1992 report entitled "The Financial Aspects of Corporate Governance" advocated the following checks and balances at board level:

- wider use of independent non-executive directors;
- the introduction of an AUDIT COMMITTEE;
- a separation between chairman and CEO;
- the use of a REMUNERATION COMMITTEE;
- adherence to a detailed code of best practice (outlined in Appendix 1).

Under the code all UK listed companies are required to report to shareholders on their governance practices, with the ultimate threat of delisting for non-compliance.

Reactions to the Cadbury Report varied. Some argued that it lacked teeth, claiming that delisting, being the ultimate sanction, would disadvantage the very shareholders who the report set out to protect, and that nothing short of legislation would stop abuses by dominant company leaders. Others feared that giving non-executives more power (Cadbury recommended that they appoint their own leader, have access to legal advice and meet separately if necessary) would erode the concept of the UNITARY BOARD, creating the continental European TWO-TIER BOARD by the back door. In the event most listed companies decided to comply with the code of best practice, except in the requirement to create a NOMINATING COMMITTEE of independent outside directors to recommend names for board appointment.

CATALYST

One role a director can play (see CONFORMANCE ROLES).

C

CHAEBOL

Large conglomerate groups of companies in South Korea, dominated by family interests, formed after the second world war with close government involvement. Recently the government has sought to reduce the power of the *chaebol* by requiring them to divest some of their interests. It has had little success.

CHAIR

Many people speak loosely of the chairman of the company, whereas his or her role is, strictly, that of chairman of the company's board of directors. Subject to anything in the company's ARTICLES OF ASSOCIATION, the directors appoint one of their number to take the chair at their meetings. There are few statutory requirements for the role so a range of styles is to be found. At one extreme the chairman does no more than manage the meetings, arrange the AGENDA, steer the discussions and ensure that they reach a conclusion. At the other extreme is the powerful chairman who acts as a figurehead for the company, influences its strategic direction and manages the board, being concerned with its membership, committees and overall performance as well as chairing board meetings.

There has been much debate about DUALITY, that is whether the role of chairman and CEO should be separate or combined. The CADBURY REPORT recommended that they should be separate; but if they were combined then the role of the independent NON-EXECUTIVE DIRECTOR should be enhanced. In Australia the roles have for many years tended to be separate. In the UK they have become increasingly separate, although a number of dominant individuals, in total command of their companies, continue to hold both titles. In the USA the predominant practice has been to combine the roles, but in the context of boards which have a majority of outside directors.

The era of political correctness has caused many organisations to reconsider the title of the chairman of their governing body and its committees. Lady chairman, chairwoman, or even the name of a piece of furniture, the chair, are used. Worldwide the number of women chairing the boards of major companies is minimal. But in many charitable and other non-profit companies, in which women play a significant board role, chairperson has become the preferred nomenclature.

The role of chairman circa AD 400:
The Abbot shall call together the whole congregation of the brethren to take council. He shall himself explain the questions at issue. And having had the advice of the brethren, he shall think it over himself, and shall do what he considers most advantageous.
Saint Benedict, *Rules for Monks*

CHINESE CORPORATE GOVERNANCE

China is providing the rest of the world with a laboratory for CORPORATE GOVERNANCE thinking. In a country influenced by Marxist thinking, OWNERSHIP is not the basis of power. But, as the country adapts to the ways of the market, advice on securities regulation, accounting standards and corporate governance is being sought and readily given by institutions and individuals from Hong Kong, the UK and the USA.

At the moment the few companies that have come to the market outside China seem to be strongly influenced by their top management. Their boards have to cope with multiple calls for control from various authorities – the relevant industry ministry in Beijing, the People's Bank of China, tax and regulatory bodies, and state, provincial and industry officials – who are concerned to avoid both unacceptable economic and social stresses such as unemployment, bankruptcy, corruption, financial pressures on the state economy and undesirable competition with state enterprises. A form of SUPERVISORY BOARD structure has been adopted, with outside members including Communist Party officials such as the local party secretary. But, as yet, their powers are in the process of definition.

Power will probably reside with top management and officialdom. The notion of independent outside directors does not seem to be a remedy for SHAREHOLDER protection, because of the lack of those with the necessary experience and power. Disclosure and accountability rules seem to offer the best hope, with the notion of a shareholders' committee to represent the interests of both international B SHARE and local A share investors.

Overseas capital is available for companies incorporated in China through two routes. The first involves a listing of the Chinese business on an overseas stock market. To date this has mainly been in Hong Kong, although companies have been listed in Australia and the USA. In Hong Kong some Chinese companies have been listed in their own right, going through the same due diligence and prospectus requirements as other companies. Others have listed through the back door by acquiring a company that already has a listing and using this as a SHELL COMPANY into which the China business is incorporated. Of course, all companies have to abide by the listing regulations of the stock exchange and the auditing and governance requirements of the Companies Ordinance. The second route is to issue B shares in China, available only to foreigners, on either the Shenzen (the special economic zone on Hong Kong's northern border) or the Shanghai stock exchanges.

CLOSELY HELD COMPANY

A PRIVATE COMPANY in which the shareholders and directors are effectively the same people. Consequently, many of the CORPORATE GOVERNANCE checks and balances that are needed to protect the rights of the SHAREHOLDER, where there is a separation between OWNERSHIP and management, are unnecessary. In some jurisdictions, such companies are exempt from some AUDIT, disclosure and filing requirements. (See FAMILY DIRECTOR.)

COALITION BUILDING

See GAMES DIRECTORS PLAY.

COMPANY LIMITED BY GUARANTEE

A type of CORPORATE ENTITY in which the guarantors agree to subscribe, to the extent of the guarantee given on incorporation, should the company be wound up. By contrast, in the JOINT STOCK LIMITED LIABILITY COMPANY a SHAREHOLDER's liability is limited to the extent of its EQUITY stake. Companies limited by guarantee are often incorporated to limit the liability of members of non-profit organisations such as academic and educational bodies, cultural and sports organisations or welfare and other charitable bodies. These companies need boards and directors, however, and most of the material in this book will be relevant to them.

COMPANY SECRETARY

An officer of the company who can, potentially, make an important contribution to the board. As the CADBURY REPORT suggested:

The company secretary has a key role to play in ensuring that board procedures are both followed and regularly reviewed. The chairman and the board will look to the company secretary for guidance on what their responsibilities are under the rules and regulations to which they are subject and on how those responsibilities should be discharged. All directors should have access to the advice and services of the company secretary and should recognise that the chairman is entitled to the strong support of the company secretary in ensuring the effective functioning of the board.

In the USA the company secretary is known as the corporate secretary. The American Society of Corporate Secretaries suggests that their duties and responsibilities include organising meetings of the board, board committees and shareholders, maintaining the corporate records and stock (SHAREHOLDER) records and liaising with the securities markets. It further states that the company secretary should be "the primary liaison between the corporation's directors and management". The company secretary need not be an employee of the company; he or she may work for an outside agency or partnership. In some jurisdictions the function can be fulfilled by another corporation. In other countries, including Australia, the company secretary must be a natural person.

The evolution of the company secretary's role reflects how much corporate life has changed. When the JOINT STOCK LIMITED LIABILITY COMPANY was developed in the UK in the mid-19th century, the directors needed someone to keep their records. This was the job of the secretary to the board. The function was largely clerical, with the directors holding the power.

This master–servant relationship is well depicted in the case of Barnett Hoares & Co *v* South London Tramways Co (1887). The company secretary of Tramways had given assurances to a contractor that sums had been retained under a contract with the company. They had not. Barnett Hoares & Co, the contractor's banker, sued Tramways for the funds. The court had to consider whether the secretary had the authority to bind the company. It decided that he did not. Lord Esher, Master of the Rolls, said:

> *A secretary is a mere servant. His position is that he is to do what he is told and no person can assume that he has the authority to represent anything at all, nor can anyone assume that statements made by him are necessarily accepted as trustworthy without further enquiry.*

A hundred years later things have changed. Corporate life has become complicated. Many companies run diverse enterprises through complex groups of subsidiary and associated companies. Legislation affecting companies has become substantial. Now the role of the company secretary calls for professional knowledge and skill.

The case of Panorama Developments (Guildford) Ltd *v* Fidelis Furnishing Fabrics (1971) shows how the courts have recognised the new situation. Panorama ran an upmarket car-hire firm. The company secretary of Fidelis hired cars, allegedly to meet clients at the airport. In fact he used them personally. So Fidelis refused to pay, arguing that, as in the Tramways case, it was not bound by the acts of its company secretary. However, Lord Denning was now Master of the Rolls. He said:

> *Times have changed. A company secretary is a much more important person nowadays than he was in 1871. He is an officer of the company with extensive duties and responsibilities. This appears not only in modern Companies Acts but also in the role which he plays in the day-to-day business of companies. He is no longer merely a clerk. He regularly makes representations on behalf of the company and enters into contracts on its behalf ... so much so that he may be regarded as held out to do such things on behalf of the company. He is certainly entitled to sign contracts connected with the administrative side of the company's affairs, such as employing staff, ordering cars and so forth. All such matters come within the ostensible authority of a company secretary.*

CONFIDANTE
One of the roles a director can play (see CONFORMANCE ROLES).

CONFORMANCE ROLES
There are two principal sets of roles that every UNITARY BOARD of directors and governing body must fulfil: conformance roles and PERFORMANCE ROLES. The conformance roles involve EXECUTIVE SUPERVISION and ACCOUNTABILITY. In recent years many of the developments in corporate regulation around the world, such as the CADBURY REPORT,

have emphasised the conformance role of boards.

The main conformance roles of directors are as follows.

Judge Directors playing this role are able to make an objective assessment of a situation. This can be a vital contribution of outside directors, who have the opportunity to see board matters from an external and independent point of view. Such an objective evaluation of top management performance can overcome the tunnel vision sometimes found in those too closely involved with the situation, or the myopia brought on by being personally affected by the outcome.

Catalyst This role is played by directors who are capable of questioning the board's assumptions and causing change in others' thinking. Catalysts point out that what appears to be an incontrovertible truth to some board members is, in fact, rooted in questionable beliefs that others have about the company, its markets, its competitors and so on. They highlight inferences that are masquerading as facts and indicate when value judgments, rather than rigorous analysis, are being used in board deliberations. Most valuably, catalysts stimulate the board discussions with new, alternative insights and ideas.

Supervisor It is the role of the whole board to monitor and supervise executive management. But the calls for non-executive directors, for a separation of the chairmanship from the chief executive responsibility and for the use of audit, nominating and remuneration committees emphasise the value of the supervisor role of outside directors.

Watch dog Directors who cast themselves in this role see themselves as the protector of the interests of other parties, such as the shareholders or, more often, a specific interest group. Representative or nominee directors inevitably find themselves in this position, as they look out for the interests of the party that put them on the board. This might be a major investor for a director on the board of an American or British listed company, the employees for a director on a German SUPERVISORY BOARD, or the *KEIRETSU* group interests for a director on the board of a major Japanese company. Every director has a duty to be concerned with the interests of the company as a whole (that is with the interests of all the members without discrimination), so the watch-dog role has to be applied with care.

Confidante Some directors may find themselves acting as a sounding board for other directors, the chief executive or the chairman; a trusted and respected counsellor in times of uncertainty and stress; someone to share concerns with about issues (often interpersonal problems) outside the boardroom. Political process at board level inevitably involves the use, and sometimes abuse, of power. The confidante can make a valuable contribution. But it is vital that he or she commands the trust of all the directors, otherwise the problem may be reinforced rather than resolved.

Safety valve It is legitimate for directors to act as safety valves at a time of crisis, in order to release the pressure, prevent further damage and save the situation. A classic example would be when the company has run into financial problems, management performance has deteriorated and the chief executive has to be replaced. Another example might be if the company faced an unexpected catastrophe. The sensible and steadying counsel of a wise member of the board can save an otherwise disastrous situation.

CONTACT PERSON
One of the roles a director can play (see PERFORMANCE ROLES).

CORE CAPABILITIES
See CORE COMPETENCES.

CORE COMPETENCES
The hidden strengths of a business that the directors can call on during STRATEGY FORMULATION. Unlike the more obvious resources that a company has, such as its product portfolio, its finan-

cial position and its organisational characteristics, core competences reflect the knowledge in the organisation and its learning capability. A core competence in a financial institution might be its strength in handling derivatives, in a software house its experience in networking applications, or in an automobile manufacturer its knowledge of electronic controls. Some refer to core competences as core capabilities, broadening the definition to include, for example, the ability of an entertainment company to deliver its video product over cable television, or of a retail chain store to access its suppliers directly by satellite-based electronic data interchange.

Strategic thinking in Western companies in recent years has emphasised the benefits of identifying the core competences and capabilities of the firm and building on them to the exclusion of all else. This includes not only the divesting of conglomerate businesses, unrelated to the core activities, but also outsourcing other functions so that both financial and managerial resources can be concentrated on the activities that are crucial to the company's strategic performance. Asia-Pacific companies, by and large, do not share this enthusiasm for concentration, tending to see business more as a series of trading opportunities which enable transient networks of inter-trading entities to be created, often with cross-holdings and cross-directorships.

CORE VALUES

A statement, typically approved at board level, of the underlying beliefs that a company has about itself and its relations with those involved with it. The core values of a passenger transport company, for example, might include statements that it is dedicated to safety, customer service and cost-effective travel, while providing rewarding career opportunities and job satisfaction for its staff, and a reasonable reward for its investors. The articulation of core values can influence the process of STRATEGY FORMULATION and POLICY-MAKING, not least because it tends to define the playing field, the games that are to be played and the rules by which the company intends to operate. (See also MISSION STATEMENT.)

CORPORATE ENTITY

The development of the corporate concept in the middle of the 19th century enabled massive capital formation, dramatic industrial development and untold wealth creation around the world. Previously, the only way to organise business was as a sole trader or partnership, in which, if the business failed, the debtor went to prison and his family to the poor-house. The JOINT STOCK LIMITED LIABILITY COMPANY enabled a legal entity to be incorporated with an existence separate from its owners, whose liability for the company's debts was limited to their equity stake. Such a corporate entity can contract, sue and be sued independently of those who have provided the capital. A dramatically simple and superbly successful concept originally, the notion of corporate entity has now become complex, with many different types of corporate structures, many forms of financial instruments and complicated international corporate networks.

CORPORATE GOVERNANCE

The way power is exercised over a CORPORATE ENTITY and the overall subject of this book. All corporate entities need to be governed as well as managed. The structure and processes of the governing body, typically the board of directors in a JOINT STOCK LIMITED LIABILITY COMPANY, is central to corporate governance. The relationships between the board and the shareholders, the auditors, the regulators and other stakeholders is also crucial to effective corporate governance, as is the linkage between the board and top management. Corporate governance is a relatively new field of study. The first book with the title *Corporate Governance* was published in 1984 and the academic journal *Corporate Governance – an international review* was launched in 1993.

C

CORPORATE PLANNING

An analytical and professional approach to the board's PERFORMANCE ROLES. Growing competition around the world during the 1960s professionalised corporate planning. Firms could no longer sell all they could produce. A market-oriented professionalism began to emerge. Management consultants offered analytical tools such as PORTFOLIO ANALYSIS, PRODUCT MAPPING, SCENARIO BUILDING, SWOT ANALYSIS and VALUE-CHAIN ANALYSIS. Corporate planning departments were created. Directors were drawn into the strategic thinking process.

CORPORATE SENATE

An idea developed by Shann Turnbull in Australia. He has suggested that "most corporations in the English-speaking world are essentially corrupt because their UNITARY BOARD structures concentrate on conflicts of interest and corporate power". His alternative is a dual board structure with a corporate senate with not more than three members, elected on the basis of one vote per SHAREHOLDER, not per share. The senate would have no proactive power but the right to veto where it feels the board has a conflict of interest. Modelled on the successful Spanish Mondragon worker co-operatives, Mr Turnbull has applied the concept to public companies he has formed.

CORPORATE SOCIAL RESPONSIBILITY
See ETHICS.

CORPORATE STRATEGY
See STRATEGY FORMULATION.

CORPORATE VEIL
A legal phrase emphasising that a company, incorporated with limited liability, is surrounded by a veil that creditors may not pierce to pursue payment of their debts from the SHAREHOLDER owners. In common law jurisdictions this even applies to subsidiary companies that are wholly owned by a parent company which controls their activities. In other words, the holding company may walk away from its subsidiary's debts. In some other jurisdictions, including Germany, creditors may pursue their debts up the corporate chain of dominating companies in a group, thus piercing the corporate veil.

CORPORATISATION
See PRIVATISATION.

CRONYISM
See GAMES DIRECTORS PLAY.

CROSS-DIRECTORSHIP
See INTERLOCKING DIRECTORSHIP

CROSS-HOLDING
The holding of EQUITY voting shares by companies in each other. The practice is prevalent in Asia-Pacific where many companies build networks of

alliances and share risk. Cross-directorships are often found where there are cross-holdings of shares. Some jurisdictions prohibit a subsidiary company holding shares in its parent, thus reducing the potential of cross-holdings. (See also *KEIRETSU*.)

CROWN JEWELS

A takeover defence used by some boards of directors of potential target companies in which they contract with another party to license or acquire a right in significant company assets. The aim is to reduce the attractiveness of the company to predators. The terms of such an arrangement allow the other party to buy out the company at a predetermined price should the takeover materialise, or obtain damages in lieu.

D

D&O INSURANCE
See INDEMNITY INSURANCE.

DEEP-POCKET SYNDROME
When a company is in financial difficulty or has become insolvent, there may be little point in shareholders or creditors suing the company because it has no money. Instead, as has become increasingly the case, their best option has been to take legal actions against those who are covered by INDEMNITY INSURANCE, such as directors and, particularly, the company auditors, to pay them what they are legally due. (See also LITIGATION.)

DESCENT FROM HEAVEN
Amakaduri, literally a descent from heaven, refers to the practice, which was prevalent in some major Japanese companies, of appointing retiring bureaucrats from the regulatory bodies to well-paid sinecures, including directorships, when they retire. The same process can be seen in other countries, including France, where members of the *Grandes Ecoles* fraternity move readily from government to corporate service.

DIFFERENT TYPES OF SHARES
Some companies create various classes of shares, under their ARTICLES OF ASSOCIATION, which have different terms such as preferential rights on a winding-up, priority to dividends, or special voting rights (see B SHARE). On the Shanghai and Shenzen stock exchanges in China "A shares" are available only to Chinese residents, whereas "B shares" are available only to foreigners. On the Hong Kong stock market "H shares" refer to shares of mainland Chinese companies listed there. (See also DUAL CLASS SHARE.)

DIRECTOR
A member of the board of directors, formally nominated and appointed by the members of the company at a properly convened meeting in accordance with the ARTICLES OF ASSOCIATION of that company. Some people may have a title including

the word director – marketing director, ASSOCIATE DIRECTOR, director of administration and so on – without necessarily being formal members of the board.

DIRECTORS' COMPETENCES

It is amazing that directors, the most important decision-makers in many organisations, often have little or no training for the job, neither are the core competences they need well understood. Apart from personality traits, such as integrity, intelligence and motivation, directors need to have basic competence in communication, decision-making, networking, political astuteness, strategic reasoning and strategic imagination. In addition, of course, all directors need to know enough about the organisation and the commercial, competitive context of the company's business to make a professional contribution. (See also CONFORMANCE ROLES and PERFORMANCE ROLES.)

DIRECTORS' CONTRACTS

It is important to distinguish between contracts that executive directors might have as employees of the company and their contracts as directors. The Greenbury Report proposed that directors' contracts should run for no more than a year (see Appendix 2). Thus directors who had performed poorly and were replaced would not receive a gigantic GOLDEN HANDSHAKE on the termination of a long-term contract. Previously many British directors had rolling contracts of three years or longer. However, acceptance of the Greenbury code is voluntary. A few companies have complied; others have reduced their directors' contracts to two years.

The pleasant but vacuous director need never worry about job security.
Warren Buffet, chairman of the Hathaway Fund, USA

DIRECTORS' REMUNERATION

This is a hot topic. Institutional investors in the

D

USA have for some years been challenging directors' remuneration packages that are felt to be excessive when related to corporate performance. In the UK the issue has come to the fore as a result of investigative journalism and SHAREHOLDER anger. Privatised utilities have borne the brunt of the criticism. For example, the 1995 AGM of British Gas, a privatised public utility, attracted one of the largest turnouts of shareholders in UK experience, one of whom brought along a pig called Cedric. The pig was named after the managing director whose 71% rise in remuneration package plus bonus, which coincided with voluntary redundancies and growing customer complaints, was the cause of concern. Nevertheless, the board, with the support of institutional investors, managed to secure the rejection of resolutions criticising its performance.

In 1995 a group of City of London institutions commissioned Sir Richard Greenbury to look into board-level pay. Details of the Code of Conduct proposed in his report are given in Appendix 2. The main recommendations were:

- companies should create a REMUNERATION COMMITTEE consisting solely of independent non-executive directors;
- the chairman of the remuneration committee should respond to shareholders' questions at the AGM;
- annual reports should include details of all director rewards, naming each director;
- directors' contracts should run for no more than a year to avoid excessive golden handshakes;
- share option schemes for directors should be linked to long-term corporate performance.

One of the problems of determining directors' remuneration is the absence of relevant benchmarks. The key criteria for any remuneration committee should be corporate performance, measured in terms of growth in profitability, business potential and SHAREHOLDER value in both the long and short term, against relevant norms that take into account the total reward structure of directors of similar companies in the same industry facing similar risks and career expectations. Such criteria should not be influenced by rewards offered to pop stars, footballers or entrepreneurs who have created their own businesses, nor by remuneration levels in other countries, unless there is a real possibility of the directors in question being able and invited to work there. In other words, the remuneration benchmarks should avoid the effects of REMUNERATION RACHETING.

To the best of my knowledge, there's no performance evaluation of boards. Directors rarely have a retreat and ask: "Let's look at the way we operate.

Warren Bennis, in "Across the Board",
National Association of Company Directors Newsletter, 1993

DIRECTORS' REPORT AND ACCOUNTS

Almost all company law jurisdictions now require the directors to submit regular reports and accounts to all shareholders (the exceptions tend to be havens such as the British Virgin Islands). Their form and content has been progressively widened and sharpened through company law and by the regulatory requirements of bodies such as the US SECURITIES AND EXCHANGE COMMISSION, the Australian Securities Commission and the Hong Kong Securities and Futures Commission.

DISCLOSURE

Directors have a FIDUCIARY DUTY not to make a SECRET PROFIT out of their position in their companies. Consequently, they are required to disclose any interests they might have in matters being considered by the board. For example, if a director had a significant stake in a company in line for the award of a contract, the director must disclose that interest. The chairman and the board can then decide whether any action is necessary, such as asking the director not to comment or to leave the room when the issue is discussed. Directors declaring an interest should always ensure that it is minuted so that their hands are clean should there be a subsequent legal challenge.

DOMINANT DIRECTOR

Sometimes a company reflects the entrepreneurial drive of one person, often the founder. In such cases the board, while able to offer advice which might be heeded, is often overshadowed by the dominant director. Bill Gates of Microsoft, Alan Sugar of Amstrad and Richard Branson of Virgin Airlines are just a few examples of dominant corporate leaders. But although dominant directors may take their companies to the highest levels of achievement, unless they can cope with the succession problem they ultimately fail. The list of those who failed to provide for their succession is endless and includes Henry Ford, "Tiny" Rowland of Lonhro and Robert MAXWELL. Unfortunately, experience suggests that dominant directors have great difficulty in working with a potential successor – "nothing grows under an oak tree". (See also DUALITY.)

> *The board's real role is to support the leader – whoever he is, chairman or CEO. If my board was absolutely divided I would put the matter to a vote: but all those who vote against me should resign.*
>
> The opinion of a dominant director

DREXEL, BURNHAM, LAMBERT

The Wall Street securities trading firm that in the 1980s was at the heart of the predator takeover market using junk bonds and was the base for the insider dealing activities of Ivan BOESKY, Dennis LEVINE and Michael MILKEN. In 1988 the firm pleaded guilty to six securities felonies and paid a record $650m in restitution. In 1990 Drexel filed for the protection of the Bankruptcy Court.

D

DUAL CLASS SHARE
Classes of shares with different voting rights are prohibited in some jurisdictions and stock exchange listing committee rules. In other cases they are utilised, often to preserve the overall power of the incumbent family or other interests when the need for additional EQUITY capital threatens to dilute their opposition below that necessary for absolute control (see B SHARE).

DUALITY
One of the ongoing debates about the UNITARY BOARD is whether the role of chairman of the board should ever be combined with that of the chief executive officer (CEO). In Australia the roles in public companies are usually separated. In the USA many major companies combine the roles. In the UK the conventional wisdom, reasserted by the CADBURY REPORT, is that it is better to have the roles separated to avoid the possibility of a strong individual unduly dominating both managers and directors. The arguments in favour of splitting the roles are that two heads are better than one, but (more importantly) that duality provides a check and balance mechanism. Shareholders, particularly if there are minority interests, may find that a dominant leader, who is both chairman and CEO, has no one to keep him or her under control. The alternative view is that single-minded leadership can produce better performance. The results of research into the alternatives seem to be that under single leadership a company can do better, at least for a while, but that where the subtle relationship between the chairman and the CEO works well, major companies thrive better in the longer term.

An extension of the duality argument is whether a CEO should ever be appointed chairman of the board after retirement. It often happens. The proponents talk of retaining his experience; the newly appointed chief executives more typically fear that, although now chairman, their predecessor may not be able to let go of the managerial ropes.

D

The classic argument against the chairman being the former CEO is that the chairman will be a meddler. The CEO doesn't need that, of course, but he does need someone to confide in, to talk candidly about changes and other important matters. People in top positions need someone they can talk with openly and honestly.

Warren Bennis, in "Across the Board",
National Association of Company Directors Newsletter, 1993

DUTY OF CARE

Most legal systems impose on directors, either through statute, case law or regulation, a duty to exercise reasonable care, diligence and skill in their work. Directors are expected to bring to their director-level responsibilities the degree of care that could reasonably be expected, given their qualifications, know-how and experience. The interpretation of what constitutes reasonable care depends on the background of the individual. If directors are accountants, engineers or lawyers, then the degree of care expected of them would take their qualifications into account. But even if they have no such qualifications, the standard of professionalism now expected of directors around the world is significantly higher than it was a few years ago. Courts can act if fraudulent or negligent behaviour is alleged or where there are apparent abuses of power or suppression of the interests of minority shareholders. For example, courts will give a ruling if it is alleged that the directors have negotiated a contract that is detrimental to the interests of the minority. But, broadly, courts will not act to second-guess board-level business decisions taken under circumstances of normal commercial risk, should they subsequently prove to have been ill-judged.

E

EMPIRE BUILDING
(See GAMES DIRECTORS PLAY.)

EMPLOYEE DIRECTOR
Proponents of industrial democracy argue that governing a major company involves an informal partnership between labour and capital, and that consequently labour should be represented in the CORPORATE GOVERNANCE processes. A German SUPERVISORY BOARD, for example, has half of its members chosen under the co-determination laws through the employees' trade union processes. In the 1970s the draft fifth directive of the European Community (now the European Union) proposed supervisory boards with employee representation for all large companies. The BULLOCK REPORT was the British response. Since then the company law harmonisation process in the EU has been overtaken by social legislation, including recent requirements that all major firms should have a works council through which employees can participate in significant strategic developments and policy changes. Most members of the EU have adopted this legislation. The UK opted-out, although the Labour Party has indicated that, if elected to power, it would reverse the opt-out decision made by the Conservative government led by John Major. Some major British firms with a presence in continental Europe have had to introduce works council procedures in their continental operations. They find there are repercussions as their British employees demand equal rights.

EMPLOYEE REPRESENTATION
See EMPLOYEE DIRECTOR.

EMPLOYEE RETIREMENT INCOME SECURITY ACT
In the USA the Employee Retirement Income Security Act (ERISA) of 1974 lays down fiduciary responsibility rules for all those who exercise control over the assets of employee retirement benefit plans. The Pension and Welfare Administration, which administers and enforces the act, has laid down criteria (in the frequently referred to "Avon

letter") which require the fund managers to act in the best interests of the plan beneficiaries, and not to use their proxy votes in companies in any way that is not in the beneficiaries' interests. This legislation also prevents directors calling on the proxy votes of shares held by their company's pension funds to promote or protect their own positions.

EQUITY

The share capital in a company that carries voting rights, and consequently the power to influence the CORPORATE GOVERNANCE of the firm. Most shares carry one vote and some stock exchanges prohibit non-voting shares and the DUAL CLASS SHARE (see also B SHARE); others do not.

ERISA

See EMPLOYEE RETIREMENT INCOME SECURITY ACT.

ETHICS

As markets and business have become global and more open to international scrutiny, more attention has been paid to corporate ethics. Well-publicised financial scandals, such as those involving Ivan BOESKY, Dennis LEVINE, Michael MILKEN and Robert MAXWELL turned the spotlight on corporate social responsibility. Environmental tragedies, such as Union Carbide's plant explosion in Bhopal, which killed and maimed many people in India, and the Exxon Valdez oil spill in Alaska, sharpened the focus. Increasingly, public opinion demands that boards of directors exercise their considerable powers for good or harm with responsibility and in the interests of the many who can be affected, rather than solely in the interests of shareholders and the short-term bottom line. Understandably, some directors feel that their job is to ensure that the company is profitable and obeys the law and that if a society wants companies to behave in a specific way it must pass legislation to that effect. But ultimately a directorship is a position of trust, demanding absolute integrity, including the ability to make moral judgments, recognising the broader societal interests that can be affected by board decisions, and distinguishing the company's interests from personal interests.

I have no problem with ethical issues, I merely ask myself whether I would mind if my old mother read about this in the press.

The company chairman of a British public company

Failed leaders were being revealed in every walk of life... sad examples of excess, greed, and cynicism... I was profoundly disappointed at how frequently the graduates of some of our finest business and law schools were involved, in one way or another, in the cases being brought before the SEC. Surely we could do better.

John Shad, previously chairman of the SEC, sponsor of the Harvard Business School's Programme in Leadership, Ethics and Corporate Responsibility, 1993

EXECUTIVE DIRECTOR

A member of the board who is also employed by the company in a management capacity. As executives such directors are employees of the company, with rights and duties under employment law. As directors, however, they are responsible like all other directors under company law: the law makes no distinction between types of directors. One of the major challenges to an executive director is to be able to separate the two roles. On the one hand to perform as a member of top management running the enterprise; on the other to be a member of the board, jointly responsible with the other directors to see that it is being run well and in the right direction.

One of the problems of a board dominated by executive directors is that they are marking their own examination papers.

Lord Caldecote when chairman of the Delta Group. Had he been commenting today, he might have added: ... and worse, many of them are awarding themselves the prizes.

Executive directors have a special responsibility to inform the board on issues where the executive has special and relevant knowledge. In addition, executives as executives have primary responsibility for managing the corporation.

The Hilmer Report, *Strictly Boardroom*, Australia, 1993

EXECUTIVE SUPERVISION

Executive supervision involves the monitoring of management performance throughout the company and is one of the key elements of the board's activities. With a UNITARY BOARD, particularly if the executive directors are in the majority or dominate board proceedings, objective monitoring and evaluation of executive performance may be diluted. Strong chairmanship of the board is then needed. With the supervisory or TWO-TIER BOARD structure this responsibility falls to the upper, SUPERVISORY BOARD. In fact many unitary boards devote the greater part of their time and effort to this function. Board papers typically report recent financial results and give recent operating data.

FAMILY DIRECTOR

A director of a company in which the controlling shares are held within a family. A family company is frequently a CLOSELY HELD COMPANY during the lifetime of the founder. On succession, however, differences can arise. Some shares may pass to members of the family that are no longer involved in management, although they remain non-executive directors. They want profits and dividends. They are concerned about expensive benefits available to the executive directors. Another conflict can arise if the second and third generations of the family expect to provide the senior management, whereas the company really needs to recruit professional management.

FIDUCIARY DUTY

Directors in all jurisdictions are expected to act with honesty, integrity and candour towards their companies, in particular towards the interests of the shareholders. This fiduciary duty is to the company as a whole, to both minority and majority shareholders, should they exist. In practice this can be difficult for a nominee director or when a dominant parent company exercises power over a subsidiary where there are minority outside shareholders. British Commonwealth-based common law (in Australia, Canada, Hong Kong, India, New Zealand, Singapore, South Africa and so on) allows directors to determine the best interests of the whole company, subject to the right of appeal to the courts. Directors of companies incorporated in the USA owe specific fiduciary duties to any minority shareholders. In other words, the primary duty of a director is to act honestly in good faith, giving all shareholders equal, sufficient and accurate information on all issues affecting their interests. The underlying (and universal) principle is that directors should not treat a company as though it exists for their personal benefit.

FIGUREHEAD

One of the roles a director can play (see PERFORMANCE ROLES).

G

GAMES DIRECTORS PLAY

Although routinely presented as a serious, analytical and rational process, boardroom behaviour is often intensely political, involving interpersonal rivalries, corporate power-plays and networking skills. The games include the following.

- **Alliance building** is a power game played outside the board room for ensuring mutual support within. It is closely allied to log rolling.
- **Coalition building** involves canvassing support for an issue informally outside the boardroom so that there is sufficient consensus when the matter is discussed formally inside the boardroom.
- **Cronyism** is supporting a director's interests even though they may not be in the best interest of the company. For example, a director declares a personal interest in a contract in a tender being discussed by the board; he might even leave the room for the discussion. Board members support his bid, however, because of their relationship, even though it is not the most worthy.
- **Empire building** is the misuse of privileged access to information, people or other resources to acquire power over organisational territory. The process often involves intrigue, battles and conquests.
- **Log rolling** occurs when director A agrees, off the record, to support director B, on a board matter concerning B, for mutual support when it comes to a matter of interest to A.
- **Snowing** involves executive directors deluging an OUTSIDE DIRECTOR seeking further INFORMATION with masses of data, thus confusing the situation and papering over any cracks.
- **Rival camps** is a game played when there are opposing factions on a board, in which hostilities, spies and double agents can be involved.

- **Sponsorship** is support by one powerful director for another, usually for their joint benefit.
- **Suboptimisation** occurs when a director argues for the benefit of part of the organisation to the detriment of the company as a whole. Some directors, particularly executive directors, suffer from tunnel vision because they are too closely involved with what is going on and from myopia because they will be personally affected by the outcome. An independent evaluation of top management performance by outside directors can help to overcome such problems.

Strong chairmanship can reduce the opportunities for game playing. (See also MEETING MANIPULATION.)

"In my experience ..." is one of the most over-used phrases in board-level discussions. The question that should always be asked is whether that experience is relevant to the subject in hand.

As they say in board meetings "trust me on this".
Peanuts

GENERIC STRATEGY
A description of the overall strategic stance of a business. For example, a company might adopt an overall generic strategy that differentiates its products or services from the competition, perhaps by product characteristics, quality, or service; or the overall generic strategy may be to focus on a specific niche in the market, a boutique operation, perhaps; or the company could rely on its scale, cost-efficiency and market positioning to compete on price with a low-cost strategy. Further, in terms of strategic options, a company may look to expand through internally generated growth and may be focused on local, regional or international markets. Or it could be genuinely global, locating procurement, manufacturing, assembly, sales and

marketing, servicing and financing wherever it is commercially and strategically viable.

GERMAN CORPORATE GOVERNANCE

Public companies in Germany have a TWO-TIER BOARD governance structure: an upper, SUPERVISORY BOARD (the *AUFSICHTSRAT*) and the executive board or committee (the *VORSTAND*). The supervisory board requires the executive board to present its proposals and plans to it for comment and approval, then reviews and assesses subsequent managerial performance. The Netherlands has also adopted the two-tier structure and it is permissible in France.

Under co-determination practices in Germany, major organisations are believed to require a close relationship between capital and labour. Consequently, supervisory boards have equal numbers of representatives of the shareholders and of the employees. Common membership of supervisory and executive boards is not permitted. The power of the supervisory board lies in its ability to appoint and remove executives from the executive committee. In the Netherlands the supervisory board has a tripartite structure: capital, labour and public interest.

Another feature of governance in major German companies is the role of German banks as major shareholders. (See case study of Metallgesellschaft, Appendix 6.)

GOLDEN HANDSHAKE

A bountiful reward given to directors on the termination of their contracts, often negotiated when the contract was first signed. Such rewards are sometimes criticised because the extent of the handshake bears no relation to the contribution the director has made to the company; sometimes the reverse. (See also DIRECTORS' CONTRACTS and DIRECTORS' REMUNERATION.)

GOLDEN PARACHUTE

A device written into some executive directors' contracts which enables them to float away from the company with exorbitant severance pay, should specific circumstances, such as a successful takeover, arise.

GOLDEN SHARE

A share in a company that gives overall power over the company to its owner, but only if a specific situation, such as a takeover bid, occurs. The most usual cases are in corporatised or privatised companies operating in fields such as power, transport or telecommunications. When privatising a public-sector business, the government may retain the right (but often for only a set number of years) to activate its golden share to stop control passing to a foreign corporation.

GOVERNING BODY

Every CORPORATE ENTITY needs to be governed and the governing body fulfils that need. In the case of a JOINT STOCK LIMITED LIABILITY COMPANY the governing body is typically the board of directors. In other corporate entities it may be called the council, the senate, the executive committee, even the governing body. Most of the ideas and insights in this book can be applied to such bodies.

GOVERNING DIRECTOR

A phrase used mainly in Australia to describe a director with dominant powers in a PRIVATE COMPANY. Although the legislation requires such companies to have two directors, the statutes do not prevent companies from framing their ARTICLES OF ASSOCIATION to give virtually all powers to one person: the governing director.

GREENMAIL

Arbitrageurs who buy shares on the possibility of a takeover bid, with the intention of bidding up the price to sell at a profit, or acquiring a sufficient stake to block the bidder and force one side or the other to buy the shares at a premium to obtain control, are indulging in greenmail.

GREENBURY REPORT

See DIRECTORS' REMUNERATION and Appendix 2.

H

HARMONISATION OF COMPANY LAW

There have been attempts in a number of jurisdictions to encourage the convergence of company law. Australia and Canada have developed business laws at the federal level, provoking adverse reactions from the states and provinces involved which argued a loss of autonomy and feared a loss of tax revenue. The European Union has also had a company law harmonisation programme for many years, although this has been largely overtaken by social legislation affecting CORPORATE GOVERNANCE issues in recent years (see also EMPLOYEE DIRECTOR). In the USA companies can be incorporated only in individual states; there is no federal companies' legislation, only securities legislation. This is one reason why companies incorporate in states such as Delaware, which have relatively liberal company laws.

HELICOPTER VISION

An essential requirement of every director: the ability to perceive issues at different levels of abstraction. When a helicopter is on the ground the pilot can see every blade of grass but cannot see very far. As the helicopter rises so more and more comes into the pilot's vision, but in less and less detail. At a considerable height it is possible to see to the distant horizon and scan all the ground in between, but the detail of individual elements has now been lost.

So it is with directors' thinking: helicopter vision involves being able to think, for example, at the level of the personalities involved in a situation, at the level of a department, STRATEGIC BUSINESS UNIT or subsidiary, or the company as a whole, or the industry, internationally or even globally. Some people, perhaps because of their professional training or earlier experience, tend to think only at a single level. They do not make good directors. Those who can perceive issues at different levels are of board potential.

But the greatest challenge to a director is not just to have helicopter vision; many people can achieve this with experience. The difficult part is to decide which level is appropriate to the matter at hand. Far too many decisions are made at an inappropriate level. Perhaps a decision is treated as an operational matter, failing to recognise the managerial or strategic aspects; or the reverse, the decision is treated as strategic, failing to recognise the operational implications.

IMRA

See INVESTMENT MANAGEMENT REGULATING AUTHORITY.

INDEMNITY INSURANCE

The need for personal indemnity against the threat of LITIGATION is becoming important in many parts of the world. Litigation brought by shareholders and others alleging misfeasance, breach of duty, negligence or other actions in damages, against companies, their boards, their auditors and, particularly, against individual named directors has been increasing. The predilection towards litigation began in the USA but has spread; auditors and directors in Australia, the UK and other countries are now increasingly subject to lawsuits that may involve huge claims for damages. Nowadays it is sensible for all wise directors to ensure that they are adequately covered by indemnity insurance. Sometimes referred to as D&O (directors and officers) insurance, such cover offers some protection against legal costs and damages awarded. In some jurisdictions directors have to pay their own premiums since, it is argued, a company may not use its own funds to protect its directors from their own negligence.

INDEPENDENT DIRECTOR

An OUTSIDE DIRECTOR or NON-EXECUTIVE DIRECTOR with no interests in the company, other than the directorship, which might affect, or be seen to affect, the exercise of independent judgment. Some regulators, such as the SECURITIES AND EXCHANGE COMMISSION in the USA, lay down detailed criteria to determine independence. Essentially, however, a director cannot be seen to be independent if he or she (or a company with which they are connected) has had significant business dealings with the company (for example, as a supplier, agent, customer, or banker), or if he or she is closely related to the chairman or a member of top management, or is a past executive of the company. Although there may be a good case for people with such connections or experience to be on the board, they cannot be considered to be fully independent, and hence cannot be part of the check and balance mechanisms enshrined in the AUDIT COMMITTEE, the NOMINATION COMMITTEE or the REMUNERATION COMMITTEE.

INDUCTION PROGRAMME

An induction programme can provide a new director with valuable INFORMATION and training. Although often "promoted" to the board for their successful executive performance, many executive directors have little knowledge and experience of board-level work. Conversely, a NON-EXECUTIVE DIRECTOR is likely to have little knowledge of the company and its industry. The purpose of a director induction programme is to speed up the time at which a director can really contribute to the board. (See the induction checklist for new directors in Appendix 5.)

> *I find that it takes a director up to a year before he really understands what is going on in board meetings, and another year before he really contributes anything worthwhile.*
> Chairman of a major UK company

INDUSTRY ANALYSIS

STRATEGY FORMULATION has to be competitor- and customer-based and is often global in context. For many directors industry analysis is the starting point for thinking about corporate strategy. Michael Porter, a professor at Harvard Business School, has outlined five driving forces of competitive analysis (see Figure 11 on the next page).

Taking an industry perspective rather than a narrower, more self-centred one, has changed the strategic battlefield for many boards. No longer are they constrained by thinking primarily about their own products and services and how to market them. Now they focus primarily on the needs of customers and potential customers. They review the strategies being pursued by their competitors. They identify potential new competitors and think about what barriers there are to entry

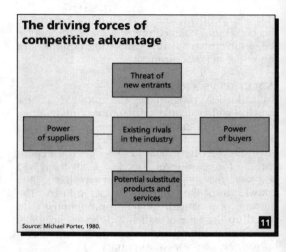

The driving forces of competitive advantage

Threat of new entrants

Power of suppliers

Existing rivals in the industry

Power of buyers

Potential substitute products and services

Source: Michael Porter, 1980.

11

into the field. They consider what developments, perhaps in technology, delivery systems or new products, might cause customers to change their allegiance. In other words, many directors are now thinking strategically, before they get down to approving plans for their own companies.

One of the difficulties of industry analysis is determining the boundaries of the industry. Industries overlap: telecommunications and computers, information technology hardware and software, retail banking and financial services. Strategic alliances increasingly cross traditional industry frontiers. Potential competitors may come from what appeared to be a non-competing industry.

INFORMATION

Directors have the right to the information they feel is necessary for them to fulfil their responsibilities as directors. Some chairmen make a great effort to ensure the directors of the company are provided with the information they need, through both formal board papers, board and individual briefings and an INDUCTION PROGRAMME. But in some companies directors are provided with no more than standard packs of data for board meetings, with inadequate information, much of which is tabled during the meeting. There are now some computer-based, information systems available that enable directors to gain access to relevant director-level information. (See also WAR ROOM.) Improving the quality of board information and an increasing use of information technology will be crucial in improving BOARD EFFECTIVENESS in the future.

INSIDE INFORMATION

Confidential information about a company's affairs known only to those inside the company. Using such information to buy shares to make a profit or sell shares to prevent a loss is INSIDER DEALING.

INSIDER DEALING

Trading in a listed company's shares on the basis of privileged, share-price sensitive INSIDE INFORMATION is a breach of a director's FIDUCIARY DUTY. It is also illegal in most countries, although it has only recently been made so in Japan, Hong Kong and Germany. But successful prosecutions for insider dealing are relatively few because it is often difficult to prove that a particular transaction was made as a result of inside information. The USA has the most severe penalties for insider dealing.

The argument against the practice, whether buying shares in the secret knowledge of events that would drive the price up, or selling shares to avoid a loss given secret intelligence on events that would cause the price to fall, is not so much that it is unfair, or because it involves a misuse of information, but because insider dealing destroys the credibility and the integrity of the market. Directors have to be particularly careful not to trade in their company's shares when they are in possession of inside information, such as the company results just prior to publication and before the stockmarket has that information. The COMPANY SECRETARY should inform directors when the window of opportunity for trading in the company's shares is open and, more importantly, when it is closed.

INSTITUTIONAL INVESTOR

A financial institution with shareholdings in listed companies, including pension funds, investment trusts, mutual funds (or unit trusts), life and other insurance companies and banks running investment portfolios for clients. The proportion of institutional investor interests in EQUITY shares has been increasing throughout the world, and in some major markets is now well over 50%. Often institutional investors show little interest in the CORPORATE GOVERNANCE of the companies in which they invest, preferring to take a short-term perspective and "vote with their feet" if they are dissatisfied with a company's performance. Some fund managers, however, have taken a stand in specific cases and voted their shares accordingly. In the early 1990s this resulted in major board changes at American Express, General Motors and IBM. Some institutions have been prominent in such developments, including Calpers (the Californian State Employees pension fund) and the UK-based Pension Investment Research Consultants (PIRC); and earlier Prudential Insurance and the British Post Office Pension Fund. (See also RELATIONSHIP INVESTING.)

> *The most important question raised by the emergence of the pension funds, and other institutional investors, as the main suppliers of capital and the majority owners of the large business is their role and function in the economy. Their emergence makes obsolete all traditional ways of managing and controlling large business. It forces us to think through and redefine the governance of companies.*
> Peter Drucker, *Post-capitalist Society*, 1993

INTERLOCKING DIRECTORSHIP

Sometimes called a cross-directorship, this is when directors sit on each others' boards. In certain circumstances, such as in strategic alliances, there can be benefits in cross-directorships. But generally the practice is suspect because of the often undisclosed concentration of power. Many studies have been done, particularly in the USA, which analyse the structure of cross-directorships. These can involve complex networks of linkages as well as direct A on B's board and B on A's board links. (See also *KEIRETSU*.)

INTERNATIONAL ORGANISATION OF SECURITIES COMMISSIONS

The International Organisation of Securities Commissions (IOSCO) is a voluntary organisation of financial regulators from over 50 countries, whose members regulate more than 98% of securities traded worldwide. Regular meetings have lead to many agreements to co-operate, including the exchange of information. Thus the regulation of financial markets and the monitoring of abnormal trading in shares have global dimensions. It is increasingly difficult to bury INSIDER DEALING through transactions in overseas markets.

INVESTMENT MANAGEMENT REGULATING AUTHORITY

The Investment Management Regulating Authority (IMRA) supervises member firms engaged in investment management and the management and operation of collective investment schemes in the UK. It also acts as trustee of regulated collective investment schemes and in-house pension funds (see MAXWELL).

IOSCO

See International Organisation of Securities Commissions.

JAPANESE CORPORATE GOVERNANCE

In the Japanese *KEIRETSU* the board plays a formal, even ritualistic role. Boards are large and almost entirely executive. Komatsu, for example, had 26 board members: the chairman, the PRESIDENT and executive vice-president, three executive managing directors, three managing directors, 14 other directors and three statutory board auditors. Canon had 26 and Toyota 55 board members. In effect the board is the top four or five layers of the management organisation. Promotion to the board, as in the West, is a mark of distinction; but, unlike the West, interpersonal competition, which has been a feature of life throughout the organisation, continues on the board for promotion to the next level. Senior managers seem often to be younger than their Western counterparts.

The commercial code calls for "representative directors" to be elected by the board. Whereas, from a Western viewpoint, these might be expected to represent the interests of various stakeholders in the firm, their actual role is to represent the company in its dealings with outside parties such as the government, banks and other companies in the industry. Typically the representative directors include the chairman and president and other top directors.

The code also calls for the appointment of individuals as full-time statutory auditors. They report to the board on any financial problems or infringements of the company code or the company articles. They can call for information from other directors and company employees and can convene special meetings of the board. These internal board-level auditors, of course, liaise with the external professional auditors.

Non-executive directors in the Western sense would be unusual. A few of the executives might have served with other companies in the *keiretsu* added-value network, and in that sense may be able to represent the interests of suppliers or downstream agents; others might have been appointed to the company's ranks on retirement from the *keiretsu*'s bankers or even from among the industry's government regulators (known as a DESCENT FROM HEAVEN). There are no independent, outside directors, no audit committees of outside directors, no remuneration committees and certainly no two-tier boards with employee representation as in Germany.

The Japanese do not see the need for intervention "from the outside". Indeed, they have difficulty in understanding how outside directors function. People who have spent their lives in a company wonder how outsiders could possibly know enough about it to make a contribution. How could they be sufficiently sensitive to the corporate culture, which has been created over the executive directors' business lifetimes? Worse, might they not damage the harmony of the group by failing to appreciate its subtleties?

Considering board styles, the social cohesion within the Japanese firm is well known. The high levels of unity throughout the organisation have been widely noted, together with non-adversarial relationships, lifetime employment, enterprise unions, personnel policies which emphasise commitment, initiation into the corporate family, cross-functional training and promotion based on loyalty and social compatibility as well as performance, even though some of these attributes may currently be threatened following recessionary pressures in Japan. Equally well known is the approach to decision-making by consensus, involving a lengthy process of discussion and negotiation throughout the organisation before agreement is reached.

The board consequently tends to be a decision-ratifying body rather than a decision-initiating and decision-taking forum, as in the West. Meetings of the entire board tend to be ceremonial, with honourable titles used on social occasions, although this aspect of society is in transition. Meetings of the managing directors with the directors in their teams are crucial. More significant, in governance practice, seem to be the informal relationships among the top echelons of the board.

*The path to the Japanese board has changed little
over the past 40 years. There is only one route
and it begins on the first day a new employee,
fresh from university, arrives at the corporate
offices... Elevation to the rank of director (is) the
supreme reward for competent service, but with
little modification in managerial
responsibilities... Eventually many departmental
heads are again promoted becoming
simultaneously head of an operating unit and a
"managing director". Even the "senior managing
directors" are heads of divisions or important
staff departments. These are masquerade boards
in which managers briefly don
the masks of directors.*

Aron Viner, "The Coming Revolution in Japan's Board Rooms",
Corporate Governance, Vol. 1, No. 3, July 1993

JOINT STOCK LIMITED LIABILITY COMPANY

A CORPORATE ENTITY formally incorporated under
the company law of a given jurisdiction, with a
legal existence separate from its owners, whose
liability for the company's debts is limited to their
EQUITY stake. It is a very simple and clever idea
from the mid-19th century which underpins
CORPORATE GOVERNANCE. Without companies there
would be no need for directors.

*Just whose liability is limited in the limited
liability company?*

A member of the Royal Family on taking up a non-executive
directorship.

The answer is the shareholders, not the directors.

JUDGE

One of the roles a director can play (see CONFORM-
ANCE ROLES.)

KEIRETSU

Networks of Japanese companies connected through inter-trading, cross-directorships and cross-holdings. Often the network includes a financial institution. Chairmen and senior directors of companies in the *keiretsu* meet regularly and have close, informal relationships. (See also CROSS-HOLDING and INTERLOCKING DIRECTORSHIP.)

L

LEAD DIRECTOR

An approach adopted by General Motors (see Appendix 3) and some other major companies, in which an outside director is chosen to chair meetings of the outside directors. Another use of the term can be found in companies with complex business interests, where individual directors are given a portfolio of interests on which they take the lead in board meetings. For example, one director might lead on new product development, marketing in a specific product group and management of one of the group's international regions.

LEGAL DUTY

Directors have two fundamental duties under the company law of almost all jurisdictions: a FIDUCIARY DUTY to act with honesty, integrity and candour towards the members of the company; and a duty to exercise reasonable care, diligence and skill in their handling of company matters.

LEVINE, DENNIS

Dennis Levine, when in his 20s, found that INSIDER DEALING was easy and apparently foolproof. As a bank employee he had access to information about prospective financial deals. Exchange that knowledge with an executive in another bank who knew about that bank's deals; open an account in a Swiss bank and trade under a false name in the Bahamas and, bingo, the compliance authorities would never know. Later, although earning over $2m legitimately from his employment with the US finance house DREXEL, BURNHAM, LAMBERT, he grew over-confident – some might say greedy. He took a position in American National Resources Company on the basis of a potential bid which his own company was preparing. He made $1.3m, but he underestimated the capabilities of government investigators and the co-operation of securities regulators (see IOSCO). Mr Levine agreed to give evidence against his colleagues, pleaded guilty and was sentenced to two years imprisonment and a fine of $362,000 on felony charges. In addition he had to make restitution to the SECURITIES AND EXCHANGE COMMISSION of $11.6m in alleged insider trading profits. Further, he had to agree to an injunction barring his employment in the securities business for life. (See also BOESKY and MILKEN).

LIMITED LIABILITY

See COMPANY LIMITED BY GUARANTEE, CORPORATE ENTITY, JOINT STOCK LIMITED LIABILITY COMPANY.

LISTING RULES

The regulations that each stock exchange lays down governing the minimum requirements for having a company's shares listed on that market. Typical listing rules include requirements on the contents of prospectuses, on reports and accounts to members, and on matters of board membership, over and above the requirements of the company law in the jurisdiction of incorporation. For example, the New York Stock Exchange requires listed companies to have an AUDIT COMMITTEE; London requires the annual report to state whether the CADBURY REPORT requirements have been fulfilled; and Hong Kong insists on two independent non-executive directors. The ultimate sanction for failing to meet the listing rules would be a refusal to list or a delisting. But since this would disenfranchise minority shareholders and penalise the market, which the listing rules are predominantly intended to protect, such sanctions tend to be threats used in discussions rather than actions carried out in practice.

LITIGATION

A growing part of corporate life. Audit firms, companies, boards and individual directors are increasingly being exposed to claims for damages in actions brought by shareholders, bankers, customers and others, alleging losses arising through negligence, usually when a company has run into financial difficulties. Courts will seldom second-guess the business judgment of boards; however, that does not prevent aggrieved parties bringing actions. In the USA, which is probably the most litigious nation in the world, the threat of legal actions is affecting the preparedness of people to serve as outside directors. Even if the INDEMNITY INSURANCE cover is adequate, directors can still face the aggravation of a legal action and the personal embarrassment of media exposure. Some companies, and particularly their auditors, having faced massive claims for damages because of the DEEP-POCKET SYNDROME, can find indemnity insurance prohibitively expensive or even unavailable.

LOG ROLLING
See GAMES DIRECTORS PLAY.

LONG-RANGE PLANNING
See BUDGETARY PLANNING.

M

MAXWELL, ROBERT

Robert Maxwell (born Jan Ludvik Hoch in Slovakia in 1923) grew up in poverty, fought with the Free Czech army and received the British Military Cross. He became an international publishing baron. In the early 1970s British government inspectors had led an inquiry into the Maxwell company Pergamon Press and concluded that he was not "a person who can be relied on to exercise stewardship of a publicly-quoted company". Nevertheless, he succeeded in building a media empire founded on two public companies: Maxwell Communication Corporation and Mirror Group Newspapers. When he died at sea in mysterious circumstances on November 8th 1991, it was alleged that he had used his dominant position as chairman of the trustees of the group's pension funds to siphon off funds to support his other interests, and that he had been involved in an illegal scheme to bolster the price of companies in the group. Eventually, the lead companies were declared insolvent and the group collapsed. Coopers & Lybrand and Deloitte Touche, called in to investigate for bank creditors, estimated that £763m had been plundered from the two public companies and their pension funds and used to prop up Mr Maxwell's private interests.

There are many lessons for directors in the Maxwell affair. Mr Maxwell's leadership style was dominant: he reserved considerable power to himself and kept his top executives in the dark. An impressive set of non-executive directors added respectability to the PUBLIC COMPANY boards, but were also ill informed. He threatened LITIGATION to prevent public discussion and criticism of his corporate affairs; many investigative journalists and one doctoral student received writs. The complexity of the group's organisational network, which included both listed entities and private Maxwell companies, many incorporated in tax havens like Liechtenstein and Gibraltar with limited disclosure requirements, made it difficult to follow transactions and to obtain a comprehensive overview of group affairs. The role of the auditors was brought into question, as were the failings of the trustees of the group pension funds. The powers and processes of the regulatory bodies, including the Department of Trade and Industry, the SERIOUS FRAUD OFFICE, the INVESTMENT MANAGEMENT REGULATORY AUTHORITY, the Stock Exchange and the OCCUPATIONAL PENSIONS BOARD, were also shown to be insufficient in practice to police Mr Maxwell's dealings.

MEETING

Directors carry out many of their functions in meetings of the board and its subcommittees. Consequently, effective meetings are crucial to board performance. Yet many chairmen fail to realise that meetings need to be planned as well as run. The AGENDA is, typically, the chairman's prerogative. (See also CHAIR, MEETING MANIPULATION, MINUTES.)

MEETING MANIPULATION

Many board meetings call as much for political acumen and interpersonal skill as for analytical ability and rational argument. There are a number of devices which the skilful meeting manipulator uses to advantage.

- At the start of the meeting, challenging the MINUTES of the last meeting can be a device to reopen discussion of an item that was resolved against your interests last time. Then, should discussion of an item in the current meeting be running the wrong way, there are a number of devices to stall or refocus the debate.
- Talking around the subject to shift the discussion on to favourable issues is a particular skill of meeting manipulators. Profound irrelevance is their stock in trade. But filibustering to run the discussion out of time will seldom work at board level.
- The put-down involves the skilful introduction of doubt when responding to a proposal before the board, as in: "We

discussed this matter before you joined the board and decided against…" or "The bank would never agree with anything like that…" These are simple examples; good put-downs can be far more sophisticated.

- Presenting ideas in the context of other people's can be powerful: "I was inclined to believe… until I heard X, now I wonder whether we should…" The fact that X was advocating something quite different is irrelevant.

- Summarising the discussion so far can be used to emphasise favourable points and downplay others: "What the meeting seems to be saying is…"

- An extension of the summarising device is to predetermine the decision, preferably in Latin, as in: "We seem to have reached the decision, chairman, NEM. CON." *Nem. con.* (*nemine contradicente*, or no one against) can be suggested, whether anyone is actually against or not.

- Where a discussion is running in quite the wrong direction: "On a POINT OF ORDER, chairman…" is a call which, if offered with sufficient challenge and conviction, will stop an orator in full flight. Strictly, points of order only have relevance if there are standing orders about the running of meetings, but that should not deter skilful meeting manipulators. Argue that the discussion has strayed from the point of the agenda item, that extraneous issues are being raised, or that this discussion would be more appropriate under another item – anything to deflect the ongoing discussion.

- Calling for a postponement of the discussion until the next meeting, on the grounds of lack of information, the need for more reflection, or until an absent member is present, can also be used to postpone a decision that seems to be running against your interests.

- Calling for an adjournment of the meeting is

a heavier version of the postponement device.

- If the ARTICLES OF ASSOCIATION or the rule book of the corporate entity specify a QUORUM, keep your eyes on the number of people present. Lack of a quorum can always be used to stymie further debate.

The meeting manipulator's advice to a new director would be to forget rationality and what you learned in your MBA programme: influence not analysis is what counts in directors' meetings. Ignore the apparent short-term issues, set out to discover the cliques and cabals, find out who wields what power over whom. Make your presence felt, but carefully: "I wonder whether we might consider ..." not "these financials are a load of rubbish". "In my experience ..." is a better start to a contribution than "Surely everyone knows that..." Propose alternatives rather than attack proposals on the table: "Another alternative might be..." rather than: "That'll never work in a month of Sundays."

MEMORANDUM OF ASSOCIATION
The formal, legal constitution governing a company. Typically, the memorandum will state the company's name, the location of its registered office, its objectives, that the liability of its members is limited and the structure of the EQUITY capital. Since a JOINT STOCK LIMITED LIABILITY COMPANY has a legal existence separate from its members, it is important for there to be a formal document that enables anyone contracting with the company to know its precise legal status. Most company law jurisdictions require the memorandum, duly agreed by the founding members of the company, to be filed at the time of incorporation. Subsequent changes require the approval of the members.

MENTOR
An experienced member of a board who accepts a responsibility, usually quite informally, to induct

and guide a new member into the ways of that board. The relationship can enable the new director to contribute more quickly and effectively.

MILKEN, MICHAEL

One of the key players in the predator takeover market in the USA during the 1980s, using high-return, high-risk junk bonds. Working for DREXEL, BURNHAM, LAMBERT, he was at the centre of the INSIDER DEALING ring that included Ivan BOESKY and Dennis LEVINE. Mr Milken and his brother were eventually indicted on 98 charges of racketeering and securities fraud. He was sentenced to ten years in prison. One of the effects of his activities was a growing interest in the way power was exercised over public companies and a new emphasis on CORPORATE GOVERNANCE.

MINUTES

The formal record of a MEETING. The COMPANY SECRETARY often keeps the minutes. Although there are no specific rules governing the content or format of minutes of board (or board subcommittee) meetings, they should provide a competent and complete record of what transpired and what was decided. Should there be any future challenge the minutes, duly approved as a true and fair report at a subsequent meeting, can be used as strong evidence of what was intended. Companies tend to develop their own minute-keeping style; for example, some boards note the names of the key contributors to the discussion, others do not. In some cases the minutes are no more than a brief record of who attended and what was decided. At the other extreme, there are minutes that are almost a verbatim report of the proceedings, complete with stage directions. The ideal lies between the two. They should contain sufficient information to capture the key threads of the discussion, the alternatives considered, the agreement reached and plans for action. The person responsible for writing the minutes potentially wields considerable power.

M

MISSION STATEMENT

A statement, usually approved at board level, of the underlying purposes of the company. A mission statement will, typically, include references to the various stakeholders in the business process; for example, suppliers, customers, shareholders, employees and, sometimes, broader societal interests. A well-developed mission statement can help the directors in the PERFORMANCE ROLES of STRATEGY FORMULATION and POLICY-MAKING, because it establishes the desired relationship between the company and other parties that might be affected by board decisions. The danger of mission statements is that they can become little more than a public relations exercise, exhorting the company to do well by all of its stakeholders without realising that their interests may be in conflict and without establishing the company's actual mission. (See also CORE VALUES.)

MONITORING MANAGEMENT

Monitoring and supervising executive management is one of the key components of a board's work. Indeed, many boards devote the major part of their time to this activity, perhaps to the detriment of the PERFORMANCE ROLES of STRATEGY FORMULATION and POLICY-MAKING. Another problem in monitoring management activity is striking the right balance between ensuring that management is pursuing the policies and plans agreed by the board, and avoiding domination of executive decision making.

Monitoring management activities often tends to be financially oriented, using data generated by the internal management accounting systems and executive information systems. But increasingly boards are seeing that they need non-financial measures of performance on matters such as customer satisfaction, product development and employee morale. Financial measures can over-emphasise the short-term performance to the detriment of the board's responsibility for the longer-term development of the business. It is also important not to rely solely on routine and standard performance reports. Briefings and presentations from non-board executives can be valuable sources of orientation and information for directors, particularly outside directors. One of the challenges executive directors face in monitoring management is that, effectively, they may be monitoring their own performance. Possible solutions are effective non-executive directors, tough-minded chairmanship and a professional BOARD STYLE. (See also EXECUTIVE SUPERVISION.)

NEM. CON.

Short for *nemine contradicente*, which means no one speaking against or unanimously (see MEETING MANIPULATION).

53% of the top 100 UK companies did not have a nominating committee in 1994 (despite the 1992 Cadbury Committee recommendations).

Richard Bostock, *Corporate Governance – an international review*, Vol. 3, No. 2, April 1995

I am not happy with co-options to the board by the incumbent directors to fill casual vacancies that are put to the AGM merely for confirmation.

John Charkham of PRONED, the official UK organisation for the Promotion of Non-Executive Directors)

NOMINATING COMMITTEE

A subcommittee of the main board made up wholly, or mainly, of independent outside directors, to make recommendations on new appointments to the board. It is an attempt to prevent the board being seen as a cosy club, in which the incumbent members appoint like-minded people to join their ranks. A check and balance mechanism designed to reduce the possibility of a DOMINANT DIRECTOR, such as the chairman or CEO, pushing through their own candidates. Nominating committees are widely used in major American companies. But it is interesting to note that the independent outside directors who form the committee are themselves often drawn from the ranks of CEOs and chairmen of other companies, and are therefore likely to recommend those of like mind. On the other hand, as some observe, if the board is to work as a tough-minded, effective team, it is just as well that its members can get on together. In the UK, although most of the proposals of the CADBURY REPORT were quickly followed by the listed companies, the requirement to have a nominating committee has met with the greatest resistance. This is not surprising since the right to appoint to the board goes to the very heart of corporate power.

N

Nominee Director
See REPRESENTATIVE DIRECTOR.

Non-executive Director
A member of the board who is not employed by the company as an executive. The term is widely used in the UK and other countries in the Commonwealth such as Australia, Hong Kong and Singapore. In the USA the term more frequently used is OUTSIDE DIRECTOR. A basic tenet of good CORPORATE GOVERNANCE is that the non-executive directors provide checks and balances on the executive directors. To achieve that, however, the non-executive directors also need to be independent of the company. In other words they should have no relationship with the company that could be seen to influence the exercise of objective, independent judgment. This means that a director acting as a nominee for a major shareholder or a bank, or someone linked to a firm in the company's added-value chain such as a supplier or a distributor, a member of the chief executive's family, or a past employee of the company cannot be seen to be independent. There may be a good case for such people to serve on the board as non-executive directors, but they cannot be seen to be independent. Particular challenges for non-executive directors are finding enough time to devote to the affairs of the company and knowing enough about the company's business and board-level issues.

Pet rocks

Ross Perot, when referring to the non-executive directors
of a large American company

*What we want are non-executive directors who
are geese not frogs. Frogs will sit motionless in
water that is heated to boiling point, unaware of
their situation, and taking no action until their
ultimate demise. Geese, as in Rome, honk loudly
at impending crisis.*

Christopher (Kit) McMahon, when deputy governor of the
Bank of England

The division of responsibility between directors, auditor and senior management, is not sufficiently clear. The focus is almost entirely on defining the responsibilities of directors. Yet the commercial reality of the matter is that, in these days of conglomerates and perhaps trans-national conglomerates at that, the opportunity for non-executive directors to exercise meaningful control over management is as slight as the ability of ministers to control a vast bureaucracy...

Justice Andrew Rogers in the AWA case, Australia, 1992

Non-profit director

A director of a non-profit enterprise (or, as some prefer, not-for-profit organisation, recognising that enterprises for profit do not always make a profit). These enterprises may be incorporated formally as companies limited by guarantee, in which case most of the material in this book will be relevant to their directors. Others may be created as trusts, in which case many of the insights and ideas can also be applied. A particular challenge to boards of non-profit entities is determining what performance measures are appropriate, given that the bottom-line profit criterion, by definition, does not apply.

Non-voting share

A share which carries rights to contribute to and participate in the company's financial affairs but not the right to vote in company meetings. Such shares are not common and are usually offered to outside investors in companies in which control is held by one shareholder (or a group of shareholders) who wants to retain a dominant position. Non-voting shares are not allowed under the LIST-ING RULES of most stock exchanges.

OCCUPATIONAL PENSIONS BOARD

An independent statutory body set up in the UK to ensure that pension schemes comply with statutory requirements and that pension schemes contracted out of the national procedures meet the minimum benefit requirements. It was caught out badly by Robert MAXWELL.

OUTSIDE DIRECTOR

A term used in North America to describe a member of the board who is not an executive employee of the company. The usage in the UK and most Commonwealth jurisdictions is NON-EXECUTIVE DIRECTOR. The term outside director tends to imply a genuine outsider, that is someone who is independent of the company, with no relationships (other than the directorship) that might be seen to affect the exercise of objective, independent judgment.

> *But what about the board? These guys were the illustrious guardians of the Ford Motor Company. They were supposed to constitute checks and balances to prevent flagrant abuse of power by top management. But it seems to me their attitude was: "As long as we're taken care of, we'll follow the leader ... There's one mystery I want to unravel before I die: How can those board members sleep at night?"*
> Lee Iacocca in his autobiography

> *The control of a large corporation is such a complex job and requires such constant attention that the outside board member, who has his own affairs to look after, can know very little about the business – too little on the whole to be useful as an outsider ... And an outside director in a large corporation cannot know enough to be specific, he must remain a figurehead.*
> Peter Drucker, *Concept of the Corporation*

OWNERSHIP

Ownership is the basis of power in the Anglo-

American concept of the corporation. Formally, the shareholder members of the company nominate and appoint the directors, who have a duty to exercise stewardship over the corporation for the benefit of the shareholders and to be accountable to them. Reality can be rather different. In large public companies the membership is likely to be diverse, with both individual and institutional shareholders, whose objectives for dividend policy and capital growth differ, and who are scattered geographically. The ability of owners to exercise power in such circumstances is severely limited. Suggested alternatives include a TWO-TIER BOARD with the SUPERVISORY BOARD reflecting, among other things, shareholder interests, or a CORPORATE SENATE providing an intermediary shareholder committee. STAKEHOLDER THEORY calls for a rethink of the essentially 19th century concept of the corporation to reflect 21st century societal needs.

> *In less than a century there is a serious question as to whether the modern corporate form has become obsolete ... How can one justify a system in which investors purchase shares in a company that is far too big and complex to permit any meaningful shareholder involvement in governance?*
> Robert A.G. Monks and Nell Minow,
> *Power and Accountability*, 1991

PERFORMANCE ROLES

The second set of roles that every UNITARY BOARD and governing body must fulfil (see also CONFORMANCE ROLES). The performance roles involve STRATEGY FORMULATION and POLICY-MAKING.

The main performance roles of directors are as follows.

Wise man This involves bringing accumulated knowledge and experience to bear on issues facing the board. The director is drawing on past experiences in business and elsewhere. In other words the board is respecting the wisdom of the director. Long-serving directors may well find themselves cast in this role by newer board colleagues. Accumulated "wisdom" can of course have limitations in fast-changing situations.

Specialist The director relies on his or her particular professional training, skills and knowledge to make a contribution. For example, the specialism could be in the realm of accountancy, banking, engineering, finance or law; or it could stem from specialist knowledge of a particular market, technology or functional area such as marketing, manufacturing or personnel. In some newer, growing companies outside directors are appointed to the board specifically to provide specialist inputs until such time as the company can afford to acquire these skills in-house at the executive level. When a board is relying on such expertise, it is important to ensure that the director remains in touch with the subject; this can sometimes prove difficult for those operating at board level.

Window-on-the-world The director is being used as a source of information on issues relevant to the board discussions. Usually this will be on matters external to the company, such as insights into market opportunities, new technologies, industry developments, financial and economic concerns or international matters. Obviously it is essential that the information is relevant, accurate and current. This is often a role specifically sought from outside directors, who are in a position to obtain such information through their day-to-day activities. A danger is that directors, the choice of whom was influenced by their access to certain information, become out of touch without admitting to their colleagues that they are no longer as close as before.

Figurehead The director is called on to represent the company in the external arena; for example, in meetings with fund managers and financial analysts, or in trade and industry gatherings. The chairman of the board often takes on this responsibility, being invited to join public committees, commissions and the governing bodies of important public institutions, as well as joining the boards of other, non-competing companies. A figurehead is also increasingly important for many companies in dealing with the media.

Contact person This is an important role often played by outside directors, who are able through personal contacts to connect the board and top management into networks of potentially useful people and organisations. For example, the director might be placed to forge contacts in the world of politics and government; link the company with relevant banking, finance or stock exchange connections; or make introductions within industry or international trade. This role typically supplements the window-on-the-world role, but adds a more proactive dimension. Many politicians are given directorships on the assumption that they have useful contacts and influence in the corridors of power.

Status provider In the past eminent public figures were often invited to join boards just to add status rather than because of any specific contribution they could make to board deliberations. A knighthood or elevation to the House of Lords, in the UK, or service as a senator in the USA, almost guaranteed invitations to join public company boards. In today's business climate, business acumen, professionalism and the ability to contribute directly to board affairs is vital. Moreover, exposure to LITIGATION deters some public figures from accepting merely honorary directorships. But even today, if a company has been experiencing some high-profile problems, it can help restore confidence if a status provider with a reputation for integrity is appointed to the board.

PEST ANALYSIS

A review of the Political, Economic, Social and Technological setting used in STRATEGY FORMULATION and POLICY-MAKING. Boards need information on the current and potential PEST context as they consider strategic options for their company around the world.

POINT OF ORDER

Some organisations establish formal rules for meetings which specify procedures for the orderly conduct of business. Typically, such rules provide for participants in the meeting to appeal to the CHAIRMAN on a "point of order" should they feel the rules are not being followed. (See also MEETING MANIPULATION.)

POISON PILL

A device for foiling a hostile takeover. For example, the terms of a company's ARTICLES OF ASSOCIATION may include provisions that:

- reduce the voting power of any shares once a holder acquires, say, 30%;
- provide a high-return security to existing shareholders should a bid not be recommended by the board;
- introduce convertible stock on which the conversion terms change on an unwelcome bid.

POLICY-MAKING

Policies enable strategies to be implemented. For example, a company may need a set of market policies that lay down the ground rules on matters such as pricing, service and customer relations. Without such policies, management might well take decisions that were contrary to the STRATEGIC INTENT. Product policies might be needed to cover issues such as product safety, innovation and quality. Financial policies might cover credit and debt collection, borrowing limits and gearing, spending controls and management approval limits, inventory control and working capital management. Employment policies might lay down the criteria for worker safety, pay and conditions, and the company's attitude towards trade unions. Some companies have written policies for social responsibility, which detail the firm's commitment, for example, towards minority rights, pollution control or the environment generally.

Policy-making is one of the key elements of the board's PERFORMANCE ROLES. In business circles it is usual to talk of policies stemming from strategies. For example, a company, having decided to pursue a strategy of product differentiation, will need appropriate pricing policies, customer relations policies and product safety policies. In government circles the terms tend to be reversed; for example, a government talks of pursuing a policy of tax reduction through various strategies such as cutting tax rates or through higher allowances.

PORTFOLIO ANALYSIS

A professional CORPORATE PLANNING technique which enables directors to locate their product portfolio in a matrix comparing market share (and thus the ability to generate cash flow) with market potential (the likelihood of growth). A jargon has grown up around portfolio methods. Firms were enabled, for example, to identify and distinguish their products as "stars", "cash cows", "dogs" and those with "potential". Star products had high market share and continuing potential; cash cow products also had large market shares but their life cycle was in decline, so they could be milked to provide the funds to invest in those products which had potential, but as yet low market share. Dogs had neither current market standing nor future potential and should be removed from the portfolio. Such methods were based on a belief that all products had life cycles, which should be reflected in corporate strategies. Experience has shown that although portfolio analysis can give directors some useful insights, it does not produce strategies. The theory of product life cycles was found to be over-simple and, organisationally, it proved difficult to find managers who were prepared to see the profits which they had created "milked" to feed other parts of the company.

PRESIDENT

A title often held in conjunction with the chairman. The precise responsibilities and powers vary considerably. It is more widely used in American companies than elsewhere.

PRIVATE COMPANY

Many company law jurisdictions differentiate between a PUBLIC COMPANY and a private company. Private companies, typically, are not allowed to make public invitations to subscribe for shares and have to limit the number of shareholders (50 in the UK). In recognition of their special status, the regulatory requirements for private companies, for example on the filing and disclosure of information, may not be as demanding. Some jurisdictions have a further subcategory of private company for the small or CLOSELY HELD COMPANY, in which the owners, directors and managers are closely related. Further relaxation of the regulatory requirements may apply, for example, over the need for AUDIT.

PRIVATISATION

Since the mid-1980s there has been a trend around the world towards corporatising and privatising enterprises that had previously been run as nationalised industries. Examples include telecommunications, power utilities, water supply, airlines, railways and shipping. The corporatisation step involves the creation of a CORPORATE ENTITY with a board of directors to run the business on market-oriented, profit-driven criteria. Typically, at this stage, the government still makes the appointments to the board and sets the investment and performance criteria. The privatisation stage involves selling all or part of the EQUITY on the stock market. Now the shareholders, who of course may still include the state, have a say in the appointment of the directors and the assessment of their performance. All the issues of CORPORATE GOVERNANCE and BOARD EFFECTIVENESS apply to privatised companies. There may, however, be an additional set of challenges brought about by the monopolistic position of, say, privatised utilities and also when there is a requirement for a privatised company to provide universal service; for example, to supply remote areas at below true market cost. Such challenges are usually tackled through the establishment of a REGULATOR, but also through government subsidies.

Privatisation is used in a completely different context to describe the actions of the directors and majority shareholders of a public listed company when they decide to make the company private by buying back those shares that are in the hands of the public.

PRODUCT MAPPING

A tool of CORPORATE PLANNING which enables directors to locate their portfolio of products, product groups or strategic business units in the context of their competitors, using whatever criteria they think appropriate, for example, by availability, distribution channels, quality, market recognition, service characteristics, or price.

PRONED

An organisation for the promotion of non-executive directors, initiated by the Bank of England and other City of London Institutions to encourage the wider use of independent non-executive directors in public and other companies in the UK. PRONED undertook an exhortatory role and provided a NON-EXECUTIVE DIRECTOR appointments service. Subsequently a similar organisation was formed in Australia.

PROXY BATTLE

In a PUBLIC COMPANY shareholders typically have the right to appoint proxies to vote on the resolutions before general meetings of shareholders. In earlier times this typically meant voting on the reappointment of directors and auditors, accepting the annual accounts and agreeing the dividend to be paid. In recent years, particularly in the USA and increasingly in the UK, dissatisfied shareholders have used the proxy mechanism to promote their concerns, calling for the removal of chairmen and chief executives, attacking the level of DIRECTORS' REMUNERATION and introducing other critical resolutions.

PUBLIC COMPANY

A company that is permitted to invite public subscription for its shares. By definition all companies listed on a stock exchange are public companies; but a public company need not be listed, attracting its shareholders (such as venture capitalists) by other means. Recognising the benefits a public company enjoys, most jurisdictions require more extensive filing, disclosure and INFORMATION access than is required of a PRIVATE COMPANY. In the early days of the corporate concept, in the 19th century, all companies were public companies. Today, although public companies tend to be the more significant firms and some of them are huge, they account for less than 5% of all companies.

QUASI-GOVERNMENT ENTERPRISE

The move towards cost-effectiveness in government in many countries has led to developments such as corporatisation, PRIVATISATION and outsourcing. One result has been the creation of various quasi-governmental institutions to facilitate, monitor and regulate these activities. Many of the issues of CORPORATE GOVERNANCE discussed in this book apply to the members of such boards, committees and councils, even though they may not have the formal title of director.

QUORUM

The minimum number of members who need to be present, under the ARTICLES OF ASSOCIATION or other rules of the CORPORATE ENTITY, to legitimise the meeting or "make it quorate". (See MEETING MANIPULATION.)

R

REGULATOR
A state-wide or federal company registrar function is necessary in all company law jurisdictions to ensure that companies are properly incorporated, listed on the company register and continue to meet such requirements as filing periodic returns and financial reports. The office of the company registrar provides one of the basic controls in CORPORATE GOVERNANCE. For a PUBLIC COMPANY listed on a stock exchange, the listing committee of the exchange also exercises a control function ensuring compliance with that exchange's LISTING RULES. Regulators are often also appointed to oversee specific industries that have been privatised.

RELATED PARTY TRANSACTION
A business transaction between a company and parties closely related to it, such as directors or major shareholders; for example, the purchase by a company from one of its directors of a building or shares in another company. The LISTING RULES of most stock exchanges require related party transactions to be disclosed and, often, approved by the other shareholders.

RELATIONSHIP INVESTING
An INSTITUTIONAL INVESTOR who takes a significant, long-term stake in a listed company with a view to being closely involved and intending to have a close relationship with the board. Examples include Warren Buffet, whose Hathaway fund invests in no more than a handful of companies for the long-term and intends to exercise some influence over the company, and Robert Monks, whose Lens Fund also takes a long-term position with a view to developing a close relationship with the company. Sometimes the relationship investor will have a REPRESENTATIVE DIRECTOR on the board. While some might argue that relationship investing represents a return to the original concept of shareholder democracy, it has to be noted that when a single investor has a close relationship with the company and is able to influence the board, the other shareholders will not have that

inside information or influence.

> *Relationship investing contrasts sharply with the stereotype of the American shareholder who is depicted as an off-track bettor with no interest in the horse beyond the results for the daily race. "Betting slip" shareholding is not a promising base for responsible ownership. The combined status of ownership and commercial relationship gives particular investors a sufficiently significant stake to ensure an effective presence.*
>
> Robert A.G. Monks, "Relationship Investing",
> *Corporate Governance*, Vol. 2, No. 2, April 1994

> *I've always said my favourite time frame for holding a stock is forever. I don't buy stocks with the idea of selling them unless I'm in arbitrage... I only invest in companies within my circle of competence: I don't mind missing opportunities from firms I don't understand.*
>
> Warren Buffet, speaking at Harvard Business School

REMUNERATION COMMITTEE

A committee of the main board, consisting wholly or mainly of independent, outside or non-executive directors, responsible for overseeing the remuneration packages of the other directors and, possibly, members of senior management. DIRECTORS' REMUNERATION has been an issue of concern around the world. In the USA it has been a particular focus of institutional and relationship investors, who have commended remuneration committees but noted the potential problem where even independent non-executive committee members are themselves executive directors of other companies and therefore have a vested interest in high benchmarks. In the UK, the Greenbury Report was specifically directed to the issue and recommended the wider use of remuneration committees. Elsewhere, including Australia and Hong Kong, there has been much debate about the extent of director rewards and the manner in which they are paid (salary, fee, bonus, options, benefits in kind and so on).

REMUNERATION RACHETING
Directors use various arguments to justify high board-level rewards.

International comparator   "To ensure that our company attracts and holds executive directors of the calibre we need against international competition, we have to pay salaries that are broadly comparable to those they could obtain in the industry anywhere in the world." This argument is advanced even if the directors concerned have never been headhunted in their lives and whether or not they have any possibility of working abroad.

Headhunter   "We have just recruited a new executive director and the headhunters assured us that he had to receive a package that is 30% more than that of the highest-paid director. Of course, we all had to have an increase to maintain differentials." This argument conveniently overlooks the fact that the fee of the headhunter is based on 30–35% of the first year's salary of the new appointee.

Top of the industry   "Our firm prides itself on being one of the leaders in the industry, even though at the moment we are not among the most profitable. We expect to pay our directors in the upper quartile of the industry range as shown by the comparator pay research." This argument totally ignores the performance of the firm or the directors.

Fear of loss   "We stand to lose our directors to the competition unless we pay competitive rates." This argument is sometimes advanced even though the directors concerned are within a year or two of retirement and would be of absolutely no interest to competitors.

Doubling up the bonus   "We believe that it is important for directors' rewards to be performance related. Moreover, we expect excellent performance in both the short and the long term. So we calculate bonuses on the annual profits, then we have a parallel three-year scheme which rewards directors if earnings per share (or profit against budget) grow by 30% over that period." This way the directors get rewarded twice on the same performance, inflation is ignored and there is no upside cap should there be exceptional circumstances. Moreover, directors do not get penalised for poor performance.

In the UK, the USA and some other countries there are now specialist consultants offering advice to companies on appropriate levels of reward. Some also advise the fund managers of institutional investors who are, increasingly, monitoring DIRECTORS' REMUNERATION and taking action when it seems out of line. (See also REMUNERATION COMMITTEE.)

> *Directors' remuneration lies at the heart of the corporate governance debate in the eyes of 90% of the British population ... Most outside directors are not remuneration experts and are conscious of the need to maintain harmony with their executive colleagues ... If governance protocols cannot be seen to tackle this problem adequately it will fail to prevent the imposition of statutory controls over the next 20 years.*
> Peter M. Brown, chairman of the Top Pay Research Group, 1993

RESPONSIBILITIES OF DIRECTORS
See FIDUCIARY DUTY and DUTY OF CARE.

REPRESENTATIVE DIRECTOR
A director who is acting as a nominee for a major SHAREHOLDER or other stakeholder, such as a venture capitalist or bank with funds invested in the company. The position of such a nominee can be fraught with difficulty because all directors have a primary duty to act for the good of the entire body of shareholders and not to take the part of any particular interested party. Furthermore, directors have a duty not to disclose privileged information

that is not available to the body of shareholders as a whole. In practice it is important for directors who have been nominated and appointed to represent specific interests that their position is understood by the other directors and, should a seriously contentious situation arise, that they take legal advice.

In Japanese company boards the concept of the representative director is the reverse; there the director is so called because he represents the company in its dealings with the government, competitors and other companies in the *KEIRETSU* network. (See JAPANESE CORPORATE GOVERNANCE.)

RIVAL CAMPS
See GAMES DIRECTORS PLAY.

ROLES FOR DIRECTORS
Although all directors have the identical responsibility to act for the good of the company, in practice different members of the board will play different roles according to their knowledge, experience and expertise. In fact directors should be appointed for the different qualities they can bring to the job, whether they are technical skills or excellent contacts. (See CONFORMANCE ROLES and PERFORMANCE ROLES.)

I no longer want to sit on large boards where the non-executive directors have largely symbolic roles. I want to learn and make a real contribution. If I take on a non-executive directorship, I will always do my best to attend board meetings, to read the papers and to take a real interest in the company concerned.
Sir Dennis Henderson

Safety valve

One of the roles a director can play (see CONFORMANCE ROLES).

SBU

See STRATEGIC BUSINESS UNIT.

Scenario building

Another tool of CORPORATE PLANNING which is used by some firms to look ahead, to identify social, economic, political or technological developments that would have significant implications for the strategic future of the firm, and to develop pictures of possible outcomes. Various techniques have been developed to produce such scenarios, including teams of experts, "futurology" and simulation modelling. Such methods are still in use in some industries, including oil and gas exploration, refining and distribution, although scenario building failed to predict the oil crisis of the 1970s, the collapse of the Soviet Union and the rapid and dramatic effects of the personal computer.

SEC

See SECURITIES AND EXCHANGE COMMISSION.

Secret profit

A director must not make a secret profit out of dealings with the company, for example through private interests in a contract in which the company is involved. Directors have a duty to disclose such interests to the board and to abide by its decision as to what is in the company's best interest.

Securities and Exchange Commission

A US body, set up under the Securities Exchange Act of 1934, to protect shareholders from over-ambitious company promoters and unscrupulously powerful incumbent boards. Over the years the disclosure, regulatory and investigative powers of the Securities and Exchange Commission (SEC) have increased and the USA now has the most expensive (and the most litigious) corporate regulatory regime in the world.

S

SERIOUS FRAUD OFFICE

The Serious Fraud Office (SFO) is the British government body that investigates and prosecutes serious or complex corporate fraud. Its success rate has not been high.

SHADOW DIRECTOR

Occasionally a company has a dominant individual, often the founder and significant shareholder, who wields power over company affairs although he is not actually on the board. For example, when new legislation was introduced in Hong Kong, requiring the disclosure of directors' shareholdings and remuneration, a number of prominent individuals resigned from their boards, thus avoiding the revelation of personal information. It was apparent, however, that they continued to exercise considerable power over the remaining directors. Such people are called shadow directors. Although they are not formally directors, the other board members operate in their shadow. In some jurisdictions shadow directors can be held responsible for certain actions in the same way as a formally appointed director.

SHAREHOLDER

The owner of shares in a company. There may be various classes of share, such as ordinary EQUITY shares (giving single or dual class voting rights), preference shares (giving preferential rights to dividend and/or on winding up) and other types of investment instrument. The vital thing for the director is to be aware of the voting rights and terms of each class, as described in the ARTICLES OF ASSOCIATION, because that determines the ultimate governance power in the company, even though crucial voting may seldom occur. (See also B SHARE and DUAL CLASS SHARE.)

SHAREHOLDER POWER

In a private, CLOSELY HELD COMPANY the shareholders and the directors are often close, even the same people, and consequently the shareholders can readily influence board decisions.

Around the commercially advanced world, however, individual shareholders in public companies seldom have real power in governance matters. In the major listed companies, shareholdings are widely dispersed and geographically spread. Even with SHAREHOLDER interest groups and better opportunities to communicate with the other members, individual investors lack the position, prestige or power to influence an incumbent chairman and the board. RELATIONSHIP INVESTING seeks to overcome this problem.

But an INSTITUTIONAL INVESTOR, even with a small holding, can influence the board, particularly if it acts in concert with others. However, the interests of different types of institutional investor do not necessarily coincide; for example, some may be looking for a quick profit, while others may take a longer-term view. There is also the potential problem, if institutional investors get too close to directors, that share price-sensitive INSIDE INFORMATION may be passed.

SHELL COMPANY

A company listed on a stock exchange whose shares are not currently being regularly traded. On some stock exchanges, if control is acquired over such companies, the listing can be used to obtain a quotation for other business enterprises without incurring the expense and exposure of a full prospectus by "backing" the other business into the shell company. This is sometimes called a "backdoor listing".

SNOWING

See GAMES DIRECTORS PLAY.

SPECIALIST

One of the roles a director can play (see PERFORMANCE ROLES.)

SPONSORSHIP

See GAMES DIRECTORS PLAY.

STAKEHOLDER THEORY

A body of ideas pursued in the 1970s and early 1980s. In the Corporate Report, a study commissioned by the UK's accounting bodies in 1975, it was suggested that major corporations had a duty to be accountable to all those who might be affected by their actions, including employees, suppliers, customers and communities, as well as shareholders. The political dimensions of the proposals resulted in considerable criticism and the shelving of the proposals. Ira Millstein and Salem Katsch, writing in 1981, offered the following insight into the issues:

> *This strident and partisan concept of*
> *substantially unrestrained corporate power*
> *and discretion is, in a more moderate form,*
> *among the most important fundamental*
> *public concerns within large corporations ...*
> *at issue is whether the nation ... will accept*
> *larger private corporate size, accelerate the*
> *decline of pluralism by regulating or by giving*
> *greater responsibility to government, or by*
> *requiring fundamental changes in the*
> *internal governance structure of our major*
> *corporations.*

Stakeholder thinking faded in the free-market, growth attitudes of the 1980s, but is now reappearing.

STATUS PROVIDER

One of the roles a director can play (see PERFORMANCE ROLES).

STEWARDSHIP THEORY

The original theory underpinning company law: directors can be trusted to pursue their FIDUCIARY DUTY to the company, acting as stewards of the shareholders' interests, which they place ahead of personal ambition. In this stewardship theory runs contrary to the ideas of AGENCY THEORY which holds that individual directors, given the chance, will maximise their own utility and cannot be expected to adopt a stewardship perspective if checks and balances are not put in place.

STRATEGIC BUSINESS UNIT
A favourite organisational approach of major western companies is to create separate organisational divisions that are strategically responsible for profit performance in specific product and market areas. The rationale is that the management of these strategic business units (SBUS), by concentrating on the performance of given strategic sectors, will maximise the benefits to the group as a whole. Doubt has been thrown on the validity of this approach by observing the practices of some Japanese companies which make the CORE COMPETENCES of the group available across the entire product portfolio.

STRATEGIC INTENT
The underlying drive of a board of directors to achieve strategic success in the longer term. It might be, for example, to become the largest company in the software industry, to be the best airline in the world or to put a specific competitor out of business. Strategic intent enables a company to make the most of its CORE COMPETENCES, to establish CORE VALUES throughout the organisation that unite everyone to the common goal, and to achieve better results than would have occurred had the board merely sought to fit the company's resources to the strategic situation.

STRATEGIC VISION
Directors need a shared perception of the future for their company; a perspective that encapsulates their aspirations for the enterprise. Some call this a strategic vision. It reflects what the board wants to achieve; the direction it wants the organisation to take; where it wants the enterprise to be in the future. "When you don't know where you're going, all roads lead you there."

Information about the strategic context is obviously fundamental to this process. One of the important developments in the provision of INFOR-

MATION at board level in recent years has been the creation of customer and competitor information systems, monitoring not what is going in inside the company, as most traditional management information systems do, but what is going on outside in the strategic milieu. Sometimes a strategic vision is articulated in no more than a general statement of overall aims; in other cases quantified aims or goals are determined.

But a strategic vision remains no more than a dream unless management can turn it into reality. Strategies have to be formulated that suggest ways in which the strategic vision might be achieved in practice.

STRATEGY FORMULATION

Setting the direction for the business, in the context of the external competitive and customer market situation, and in the light of prevailing economic, political and technological factors. This is a crucial aspect of the board's role; it is after all why directors are so called.

Strategy formulation is typically an iterative process leading from perceptions of the strategic situation, through possible strategies, choices, projects, plans, implementation and outcomes. Strategic thinking is ongoing. Strategies tend to emerge over time rather than be created by a deliberate planning process.

During the 1970s and 1980s it became apparent that companies with highly sophisticated CORPORATE PLANNING methods were not necessarily the most strategically successful. Competitors, often from Japan or elsewhere in Asia-Pacific, seemed to be achieving global prominence without the formal, analytical approaches to corporate planning that many western companies used. Conventional assumptions about formal corporate planning came in for a reappraisal.

The crucial discovery, which had been known by military strategists for thousands of years, was that it is not possible to create strategies for an organisation until the strategies being pursued (and capable of being pursued) by rival (and potential rival) organisations are understood. Company-centred planning systems and the tools of professional corporate planning had failed to adopt this perspective. HELICOPTER VISION is needed to see the business in the context of its competitors and customers, and of the political, economic, social, and technological setting (see PEST). INDUSTRY ANALYSIS is needed.

Alternative strategies need to be developed, evaluated and, eventually, choices have to be made by the directors. Then the chosen strategies need supporting by appropriate POLICY-MAKING that lays down the guidelines for management. In formulating strategy and making related policy, a particular challenge to directors is to ensure that the long-term interests of the company are balanced with the short-term interests. Pressure to show strong performance in annual (even quarterly) directors' reports can all too easily adversely affect the pursuit of strategies that would fit the company for a better strategic future.

A significant trend in recent years has been away from strategies that emphasise business as a battlefield with global competitors and towards searching out strategic allies with whom mutually beneficial strategic alliances can be built. Major companies in the computer hardware industry, for example, have created hundreds of alliances with peripheral equipment manufacturers, software houses, and information service and entertainment providers.

In earlier days, when change and strategic challenge came relatively slowly, corporate planning was often an annual process, associated with the budget preparation. Today, strategy formulation, in most professionally led companies, is a constant activity for top management and the directors. Strategies tend to emerge as a stream of strategically significant information is digested and strategic options are discussed. Some boards of directors delegate much of the strategy formulation to the chief executive and top management. The outside directors act more as catalysts, probing the management's proposals, questioning their assumptions, challenging their conclusions, until a consensus is reached. Other boards are more closely involved in the details of strategic thinking. Recognising the importance of board-led strategic thinking, directors seem increasingly to be devoting specific board time and effort to strategy formulation, both during board meetings and by creating specific strategy sessions, often away from the boardroom.

In entrepreneurial firms strategies are often hidden and success often stems from unexpected and innovative strategies initiated by a dominant figure who has the ability to recognise strategic opportunities and seize them quickly. The boards of such companies are generally happy to give entrepreneurial business leaders the support they feel they need – at least for as long as the company continues its strategic success.

All men can see the tactics whereby I conquer: but none can see the strategy out of which victory is evolved.
Sun Tze, *The Art of War*, 6th century BC

The board of a large public corporation is an inappropriate body for developing strategy, setting corporate culture and policy and initiating major decisions. Instead the board should concentrate on the critical review of proposals, with management having the primary duty to formulate and then implement proposals.
The Hilmer Report, *Strictly Boardroom*, Australia 1993

SUBOPTIMISATION
See GAMES DIRECTORS PLAY.

SUPERVISOR
One of the roles a director can play (see CONFORMANCE ROLES).

SUPERVISORY BOARD
The upper board in the TWO-TIER BOARD approach to CORPORATE GOVERNANCE. In the continental Euro-

pean model, the supervisory board monitors and supervises the performance of the executive board. Its power is derived from the ability to hire and fire the chief executive and other members of the executive. Membership of both the supervisory board and the executive board is not allowed. Some protagonists argue that the supervisory board distinguishes CONFORMANCE ROLES and PERFORMANCE ROLES that can become confused in a UNITARY BOARD. The critics of supervisory boards point out some of those that have failed, such as the Metallgesellschaft supervisory board, which was unable to detect the exposure to derivative trading in its US subsidiary, nearly causing the group to fail (see Appendix 6). (See also *AUFSICHT-SRAT* and *VORSTAND*.)

In designing systems of CORPORATE GOVERNANCE for state companies to be listed on overseas stock exchanges, the authorities in China adopted a unitary board (of executive and non-executive directors) to run the business plus a supervisory board to exercise oversight. However, the supervisory board is not exactly a two-tier board structure with the supervisory board on top, because power also stems from the central government authorities and the Communist Party apparatus.

SWOT ANALYSIS
A favourite analytical tool of CORPORATE PLANNING which involves taking a rigorous review of the Strengths and Weaknesses that the company has and the Opportunities and Threats that it faces. This technique is still used by many boards today. As a vehicle for focusing directors' attention on crucial strategic issues and building up their knowledge of the company's situation, SWOT analysis has value. Its fundamental weakness is that it is company-centred; that is the strategic thinkers are, as it were, sitting inside the company looking out. True strategic thinking requires the strategist to be able to perceive the company in the context of its industry, customers and competitors (see HELICOPTER VISION).

TITLES

Not all people who carry the title of director are directors; and some who do not bear the title director may be held liable as though they were. Titles such as director of long range planning or director of private banking business may be useful to add status to the post, but do not necessarily imply membership of the board of directors. Such people would be associate directors. On the other hand, shadow directors are those who, while not formally having the title of director, influence board decisions. They may be held responsible, in law, for the exercise of that power.

TOKENISM

The inclusion of people on PUBLIC COMPANY boards of directors because they reflect (and can be seen to reflect) stakeholder interests such as gender, race or other minority concerns, rather than because of the specific contribution they can make to the board's work. Tokenism was at its height during the stakeholder debates of the 1970s, particularly among top US corporations. Today nomination committees that recommend women or members of other interest groups do so primarily because of their potential to contribute to the board's work, and not merely as a gesture to stakeholder groups.

The same reason which induced the Romans to have two consuls makes it desirable for there to be two chambers of parliament; that neither of them may be exposed to the corrupting influence of undivided power...
John Stewart Mill

TWO-TIER BOARDS

A governance structure found in continental European countries, such as Germany and the Netherlands, in which the executive board comprising the top executive team is entirely separate from the upper SUPERVISORY BOARD. (See also *AUFSICHTSRAT* and *VORSTAND*.)

UNITARY BOARD

Companies incorporated in the USA, the UK and other Commonwealth company law jurisdictions have boards with both executive and outside, non-executive directors. By contrast, companies incorporated in some continental European jurisdictions have a TWO-TIER BOARD. The unitary board can comprise entirely executive directors, have a minority or majority of outside, non-executive directors, or be composed entirely of non-executive directors.

VICE-CHAIR

A title used by some boards to spread the workload of the chairman; by others to mark the chairman-elect; and by yet others to confer prestige without necessarily giving additional responsibilities or powers (see CHAIR).

> *Chairman, Vice-chairman, President – the titles do not always mean quite what they seem. Analysing the hierarchies at the top of American public companies can be a little like working out where real power lies in the Kremlin. The man at the top of the pecking order may, indeed, be the big potato, but it is just as likely that he counts for nothing at all.*
>
> Robert Lacey, *Detroit's Destiny*

VOLUNTARY ORGANISATIONS' GOVERNANCE

See NON-PROFIT DIRECTOR.

VORSTAND

The executive committee or board in the German TWO-TIER BOARD system of corporate governance.

VOTING RIGHTS

The ARTICLES OF ASSOCIATION usually provide the terms and procedures for members' voting in general meetings of a company. If those attending a meeting vote by a show of hands, the size of individual shareholdings will not count; but if a poll is called for, the typical clause in the articles provides for one vote for each share. (See EQUITY and DUAL CLASS SHARE.)

VOTING WITH THEIR FEET

The tendency of some institutional investors to prefer not to become involved in the governance issues of companies in which they have invested; in other words selling their shares rather than engaging in a PROXY BATTLE. (See also RELATIONSHIP INVESTING.)

W

WAR ROOM
Some boards have their boardrooms fitted out with display screens and information-retrieval facilities to provide information pertinent to decisions under discussion. The analogy with the military operations room in a battle situation is, however, suspect since military operations involve real-time tactical responses as situations evolve, whereas the time horizon of board-level decisions tends to be long-term strategic.

WATCHDOG
One of the roles a director can play (see CONFORMANCE ROLES.)

WINDOW-ON-THE-WORLD
One of the roles a director can play (see PERFORMANCE ROLES.)

WISE MAN
One of the roles a director can play (see PERFORMANCE ROLES.)

Women directors used to be in politics or good works: today they are younger, with relevant business experience.
Viki Holton, *Corporate Governance – an international review*, Vol. 3, No. 2, April 1995

WOMAN DIRECTOR
Research has shown more women than ever before are reaching the top levels of the major UK organisations; but although the number of individuals in the group has increased, a statistic that has remained constant is that just over 80% of women directors are non-executives. Only 11 women identified in a 1993 survey are executive directors, and only one has the most senior job in the company. Assuming the rate of progress seen between 1989 and 1994, it will not be before the year 2017 that there is at least one woman on the board of each of the Times Top 200 British companies.

WORKER DIRECTOR
See EMPLOYEE DIRECTOR.

WORKS COUNCIL
See EMPLOYEE DIRECTOR.

YAKUSA

Japanese gangster organisations, often run in a business-like, corporate manner. The *yakusa* sometimes threaten disruption of companies' AGMs if they are not suitably rewarded. Consequently, many companies hold their AGMs on the same day. Links were found by a parliamentary committee in 1991 between a *yakusa* organisation and Nomura and Nikko securities companies, when it was alleged that they had helped the mobsters inflate the value of a railway company's stock for their own benefit.

Z

ZAIBATSU

Closely related networks of Japanese companies which operated in the early years of the 20th century. After the second world war the occupying forces sought to disband the *zaibatsu* because of their previous close connections with military central powers. They were only partially successful and some of the *KEIRETSU* reflect the earlier relationships.

Part 3

APPENDIXES

1 The Cadbury Report

The Code of Best Practice
(on the financial aspects of corporate
governance)

1 THE BOARD OF DIRECTORS

1.1 The board should meet regularly, retain full
and effective control over the company and
monitor the executive management.

1.2 There should be a clearly accepted division
of responsibilities at the head of a company,
which will ensure a balance of power and
authority, such that no one individual has
unfettered powers of decision. Where the
chairman is also the chief executive, it is essential
that there should be a strong and independent
element on the board, with a recognised senior
member.

1.3 The board should include non-executive
directors of sufficient calibre and number for
their views to carry significant weight in the
board's decisions.

1.4 The board should have a formal schedule of
matters specifically reserved to it for decision to
ensure that the direction and control of the
company is firmly in its hands.

1.5 There should be an agreed procedure for
directors in the furtherance of their duties to take
independent professional advice if necessary, at
the company's expense.

1.6 All directors should have access to the
advice and services of the company secretary,
who is responsible to the board for ensuring that
board procedures are followed and that
applicable rules and regulations are complied
with. Any question of the removal of the

company secretary should be a matter for the
board as a whole.

2 NON-EXECUTIVE DIRECTORS

2.1 Non-executive directors should bring an
independent judgment to bear on issues of
strategy, performance, resources, including key
appointments, and standards of conduct.

2.2 The majority should be independent of
management and free from any business or other
relationship which could materially interfere with
the exercise of their independent judgment, apart
from their fees and shareholding. Their fees
should reflect the time which they commit to the
company.

2.3 Non-executive directors should be appointed
for specified terms and reappointment should not
be automatic.

2.4 Non-executive directors should be selected
through a formal process and both this process
and their appointment should be a matter for the
board as a whole.

3 EXECUTIVE DIRECTORS

3.1 Directors' service contracts should not
exceed three years without shareholders'
approval.

3.2 There should be full and clear disclosure of
directors' total emoluments and those of the
chairman and highest-paid director, including
pension contributions and stock options.
Separate figures should be given for salary and
performance-related elements and the basis on
which performance is measured should be
explained.

3.3 Executive directors' pay should be subject to the recommendations of a remuneration committee made up wholly or mainly of non-executive directors.

4 REPORTING AND CONTROLS

4.1 It is the board's duty to present a balanced and understandable assessment of the company's position.

4.2 The board should ensure that an objective and professional relationship is maintained with the auditors.

4.3 The board should establish an audit committee of at least three non-executive directors with written terms of reference which deal clearly with its authority and duties.

4.4 The directors should explain their responsibility for preparing the accounts next to a statement by the auditors about their reporting responsibilities.

4.5 The directors should report on the effectiveness of the company's system of internal control.

4.6 The directors should report that the business is a going concern, with supporting assumptions or qualifications as necessary.

Reproduced with the permission of the publishers, Gee and Co, South Quay Plaza, 183 Marsh Wall, London E14 9FS

2 The Greenbury Report

The Code of Best Practice
(on directors' remuneration)

INTRODUCTION

1 The purpose of the accompanying code is to set out best practice in determining and accounting for directors' remuneration.

2 The detailed provisions have been prepared with large companies mainly in mind, but the principles apply equally to smaller companies.

3 We recommend that all listed companies registered in the UK should comply with the code to the fullest extent practicable and include a statement about their compliance in the annual reports to shareholders by their remuneration committees or elsewhere in their annual reports and accounts. Any areas of non-compliance should be explained and justified.

4 We further recommend that the London Stock Exchange should introduce the following continuing obligations for listed companies:

- an obligation to include in their annual remuneration committee reports to shareholders or their annual reports a general statement about their compliance with section A of the code which should also explain and justify and areas of non-compliance;
- a specific obligation to comply with the provisions in section B of the code which are not already covered by existing obligations, and with provision C10 of the code, subject to any changes of wording which may be desirable for legal or technical reasons.

5 Within section B, provision B3 requires remuneration committees to confirm that full consideration has been given to sections C and D of the code.

THE CODE

A The remuneration committee

A1 To avoid potential conflicts of interest, boards of directors should set up remuneration committees of non-executive directors to determine on their behalf, and on behalf of the shareholders, within agreed terms of reference, the company's policy on executive remuneration and specific remuneration packages for each of the executive directors, including pension rights and any compensation payments.

A2 Remuneration committee chairmen should account directly to the shareholders through the means specified in this code for the decisions their committees reach.

A3 Where necessary, companies' articles of association should be amended to enable remuneration committees to discharge these functions on behalf of the board.

A4 Remuneration committees should consist exclusively of non-executive directors with no personal financial interest other than as shareholders in the matters to be decided, no potential conflicts of interest arising from cross-directorships and no day-to-day involvement in running the business.

A5 The members of the remuneration committee should be listed each year in the committee's report to shareholders (B1 below). When they stand for re-election, the proxy cards should indicate their membership of the committee.

A6 The board itself should determine the remuneration of the non-executive directors, including members of the remuneration committee, within the limits set in the articles of association.

A7 Remuneration committees should consult the company chairman and/or chief executive about their proposals and have access to professional advice inside and outside the company.

A8 The remuneration committee chairman should attend the company's annual general meeting (AGM) to answer shareholders' questions about directors' remuneration and should ensure that the company maintains contact as required with its principal shareholders about remuneration in the same way as for other matters.

A9 The committee's annual report to shareholders (B1 below) should not be a standard item of agenda for AGMs. But the committee should consider each year whether the circumstances are such that the AGM should be invited to approve the policy set out in their report and should minute their conclusions.

B DISCLOSURE AND APPROVAL PROVISIONS

B1 The remuneration committee should make a report each year to the shareholders on behalf of the board. The report should form part of, or be annexed to, the company's annual report and accounts. It should be the main vehicle through which the company accounts to shareholders for directors' remuneration.

B2 The report should set out the company's policy on executive directors' remuneration, including levels, comparator groups of companies, individual components, performance criteria and measurement, pension provision, contracts of service and compensation commitments on early termination.

B3 The report should state that, in framing its remuneration policy, the committee has given full consideration to the best practice provisions set out in sections C and D below.

B4 The report should also include full details of all elements in the remuneration package of each individual director by name, such as basic salary, benefits in kind, annual bonuses and long-term incentive schemes including share options.

B5 Information on share options, including save as you earn (SAYE) options, should be given for each director in accordance with the recommendations of the Accounting Standards Board's Urgent Issues Task Force Abstract 10 and its successors.

B6 If grants under executive share option or other long-term incentive schemes are awarded in one large block rather than phased, the report should explain and justify.

B7 Also included in the report should be pension entitlements earned by each individual director during the year, calculated on a basis to be recommended by the Faculty of Actuaries and the Institute of Actuaries.

B8 If annual bonuses or benefits in kind are pensionable the report should explain and justify.

B9 The amounts received by, and commitments made to, each director under B4, B5 and B7 should be subject to audit.

B10 Any service contracts which provide for, or imply, notice periods in excess of one year (or any provisions for predetermined compensation on termination which exceed one year's salary and benefits) should be disclosed and the reasons for the longer notice periods explained.

B11 Shareholdings and other relevant business interests and activities of the directors should continue to be disclosed as required in the Companies Acts and London Stock Exchange Listing Rules.

B12 Shareholders should be invited specifically to approve all new long-term incentive schemes (including share-option schemes) whether payable in cash or shares in which directors or senior executives will participate which potentially commit shareholders' funds over more than one year or dilute the equity.

C REMUNERATION POLICY

C1 Remuneration committees must provide the packages needed to attract, retain and motivate directors of the quality required but should avoid paying more than is necessary for this purpose.

C2 Remuneration committees should judge where to position their company relative to other companies. They should be aware what other comparable companies are paying and should take account of relative performance.

C3 Remuneration committees should be sensitive to the wider scene, including pay and employment conditions elsewhere in the company, especially when determining annual salary increases.

C4 The performance-related elements of remuneration should be designed to align the interests of directors and shareholders and to give directors keen incentives to perform at the highest levels.

C5 Remuneration committees should consider whether their directors should be eligible for annual bonuses. If so, performance conditions should be relevant, stretching and designed to enhance the business. Upper limits should always be considered. There may be a case for part-payment in shares to be held for a significant period.

C6 Remuneration committees should consider whether their directors should be eligible for benefits under long-term incentive schemes. Traditional share-option schemes should be weighed against other kinds of long-term incentive schemes. In normal circumstances, shares granted should not vest, and options should not be exercisable, in under three years. Directors should be encouraged to hold their shares for a further period after vesting or exercise subject to the need to finance any costs of acquisition and associated tax liability.

C7 Any new long-term incentive schemes which are proposed should preferably replace existing schemes or at least form part of a well-considered overall plan, incorporating existing schemes, which should be approved as a whole by shareholders. The total rewards potentially available should not be excessive. (See also B12.)

C8 Grants under all incentive schemes, including new grants under existing share option schemes, should be subject to challenging performance criteria reflecting the company's objectives. Consideration should be given to criteria which reflect the company's performance relative to a group of comparator companies in some key variables such as total shareholder return.

C9 Grants under executive share-option and other long-term incentive schemes should normally be phased rather than awarded in one large block. (See B6.)

C10 Executive share options should never be issued at a discount.

C11 Remuneration committees should consider the pension consequences and associated costs to the company of basic salary increases, especially for directors close to retirement.

C12 In general, neither annual bonuses nor benefits in kind should be pensionable. (See B8.)

D SERVICE CONTRACTS AND COMPENSATION

D1 Remuneration committees should consider what compensation commitments their directors' contracts of service, if any, would entail in the event of early termination, particularly for unsatisfactory performance.

D2 There is a strong case for setting notice or contract periods at, or reducing them to, one year or less (see B10). Remuneration committees should, however, be sensitive and flexible, especially over timing. In some cases notice or contract periods of up to two years may be acceptable. Longer periods should be avoided wherever possible.

D3 If it is necessary to offer longer notice or contract periods, such as three years, to new directors recruited from outside, such periods should reduce after the initial period.

D4 Within the legal constraints, remuneration committees should tailor their approach in individual early termination cases to the wide variety of circumstances. The broad aim should be to avoid rewarding poor performance while dealing fairly with cases where departure is not due to poor performance.

D5 Remuneration committees should take a robust line on payment of compensation where performance has been unsatisfactory and on reducing compensation to reflect departing directors' obligations to mitigate damages by earning money elsewhere.

D6 Where appropriate, and in particular where notice or contract periods exceed one year, companies should consider paying all or part of compensation in instalments rather than one lump sum and reducing or stopping payment when the former director takes on new employment.

Reproduced with the permission of the publishers, Gee and Co, South Quay Plaza, 183 Marsh Wall, London E14 9FS

3 General Motors Corporation

In a message to stockholders of General Motors in 1994, the chairman, John Smale, wrote:

> The management of General Motors has been charged by your board of directors to ensure the successful perpetuation of the business, while recognising the corporation's responsibilities to its customers, employees, communities, dealers, and suppliers. To prosper in our increasingly global competitive markets will require innovative and bold thinking, risk taking, and altering strategies when necessary. It is a management task requiring discipline and dedication.
>
> Your board of directors is responsible to you, the stockholders of General Motors, to have in place the best management team it can develop; to help that team set the goals and priorities for the long term designed to successfully perpetuate the business; to see that management has the incentive to achieve those goals and priorities; and then to regularly monitor management's accomplishments against those goals and priorities.
>
> To meet that responsibility, the board's 12 outside directors spent all or part of 24 days last year, in addition to preparation, on the affairs of the corporation. The outside directors take key roles in such crucial committees as capital stock, finance, audit, public policy, incentive and compensation, and director affairs.
>
> During the past year, the General Motors board has re-examined its processes and has established a set of operating guidelines which will ensure that it is performing its responsibilities with the same discipline and dedication that it expects of management…

The following guidelines for the board were adopted in January 1994 and revised in August 1995.

GUIDELINES ON SIGNIFICANT CORPORATE GOVERNANCE ISSUES

Selection and composition of the board

1 Board membership criteria

The committee on director affairs is responsible for reviewing with the board, on an annual basis, the appropriate skills and characteristics required of board members in the context of the current make-up of the board. This assessment should include issues of diversity, age, skills such as understanding of manufacturing technologies, international background, etc – all in the context of an assessment of the perceived needs of the board at that point in time.

2 Selection and orientation of new directors

The board itself should be responsible, in fact as well as procedure, for selecting its own members and in recommending them for election by the stockholders. The board delegates the screening process involved to the committee on director affairs with the direct input from the chairman of the board as well as the chief executive officer. The board and the company have a complete orientation process for new directors that includes background material, meetings with senior management and visits to company facilities.

3 Extending the invitation to a potential director to join the board

The invitation to join the board should be extended by the board itself, by the chairman of the committee on director affairs (if the chairman and chief executive officer hold the same position), the chairman of the board, and the chief executive officer of the company.

Board leadership

4 Selection of chairman and chief executive officer

The board should be free to make this choice

any way that seems best for the company at a given point in time.

Therefore, the board does not have a policy, one way or the other, on whether or not the role of the chief executive and chairman should be separate and, if it is to be separate, whether the chairman should be selected from the non-employee directors or be an employee.

5 Lead director concept

The board adopted a policy that it have a director selected by the outside directors who will assume the responsibility of chairing the regularly scheduled meetings of outside directors or other responsibilities which the outside directors as a whole might designate from time to time.

Currently, this role is filled by the non-executive chairman of the board. Should the company be organised in such a way that the chairman is an employee of the company, another director would be selected for this responsibility.

Board composition and performance

6 Size of the board

The board presently has 13 members. It is the sense of the board that a size of about 15 is about right. However, the board would be willing to go to a somewhat larger size in order to accommodate the availability of an outstanding candidate(s).

7 Mix of inside and outside directors

The board believes that as a matter of policy there should be a majority of independent directors on the GM board (as stipulated in Bylaw 2.12). The board is willing to have members of management, in addition to the chief executive officer, as directors. But the board believes that management should encourage senior managers to understand that board membership is not necessary or a prerequisite to any higher management position in the company. Managers other than the chief executive officer currently attend board meetings on a regular basis even though they are not members of the board.

On matters of corporate governance, the board assumes decisions will be made by the outside directors.

8 Board definition of what constitutes independence for outside directors

GM's Bylaw defining independent directors was approved by the board in January 1991. The board believes there is no current relationship between any outside director at GM that would be construed in any way to compromise any board member being designated independent. Compliance with the Bylaw is reviewed annually by the committee on director affairs.

9 Former chief executive officer's board membership

The board believes this is a matter to be decided in each individual instance. It is assumed that when the chief executive officer resigns from that position, he/she should offer his/her resignation from the board at the same time. Whether the individual continues to serve on the board is a matter for discussion at that time with the new chief executive officer and the board.

A former chief executive officer serving on the board will be considered an inside director for purposes of corporate governance.

10 Directors who change their present job responsibility

It is the sense of the board that individual directors who change the responsibility they held when they were elected to the board should submit a letter of resignation to the board.

It is not the sense of the board that in every instance the directors who retire or change from the position they held when they came on the board should necessarily leave the board. There should, however, be an opportunity for the board, via the committee on director affairs, to review the continued appropriateness of board membership under these circumstances.

11 Term limits

The board does not believe it should establish term limits. While term limits could help insure that there are fresh ideas and viewpoints available to the board, they hold the disadvantage of losing the contribution of directors who have been able to develop, over a period of time, increasing insight into the company and its operations and, therefore, provide an increasing contribution to the board as a whole.

As an alternative to term limits, the committee on director affairs, in conjunction with the chief executive officer and the chairman of the board, will formally review each director's continuation on the board every five years. This will also allow each director the opportunity to conveniently confirm his/her desire to continue as a member of the board.

12 Retirement age

It is the sense of the board that the current retirement age of 70 is appropriate.

13 Board compensation review

It is appropriate for the staff of the company to report once a year to the committee on director affairs the status of GM board compensation in relation to other large US companies. As part of a director's total compensation and to create a direct linkage with corporate performance, the board believes that a meaningful portion of a director's compensation should be provided in common stock units.

Changes in board compensation, if any, should come at the suggestion of the committee on director affairs, but with full discussion and concurrence by the board.

14 Executive sessions of outside directors
The outside directors of the board will meet in executive session three times each year. The format of these meetings will include a discussion with the chief executive officer on each occasion.

15 Assessing the board's performance
The committee on director affairs is responsible to report annually to the board an assessment of the board's performance. This will be discussed with the full board. This should be done following the end of each fiscal year and at the same time as the report on board membership criteria.

This assessment should be of the board's contribution as a whole and specifically review areas in which the board and/or the management believes a better contribution could be made. Its purpose is to increase the effectiveness of the board, not to target individual board members.

16 Board interaction with institutional investors, the press, customers, etc
The board believes that the management speaks for General Motors. Individual board members may, from time to time at the request of the management, meet or otherwise communicate with various constituencies that are involved with General Motors. If comments from the board are appropriate, they should, in most circumstances, come from the chairman.

Board relationship to senior management

17 Regular attendance of non-directors at board meetings
The board welcomes the regular attendance at each board meeting of non-board members who are members of the president's council.

Should the chief executive officer want to add additional people as attendees on a regular basis, it is expected that this suggestion would be made to the board for its concurrence.

18 Board access to senior management
Board members have complete access to GM's management.

It is assumed that board members will use judgment to be sure that this contact is not distracting to the business operation of the company and that such contact, if in writing, be copied to the chief executive and the chairman.

Furthermore, the board encourages the management to, from time to time, bring managers into board meetings who: (a) can provide additional insight into the items being discussed because of personal involvement in these areas; and/or (b) represent managers with future potential that the senior management believes should be given exposure to the board.

Meeting procedures

19 Selection of agenda items for board meetings
The chairman of the board and the chief executive officer (if the chairman is not the chief executive officer) will establish the agenda for each board meeting.

Each board member is free to suggest the inclusion of item(s) on the agenda.

20 Board materials distributed in advance
It is the sense of the board that information and data that is important to the board's understanding of the business be distributed in writing to the board before the board meets. The management will make every attempt to see that this material is as brief as possible while still providing the desired information.

21 Board presentations
As a general rule, presentations on specific subjects should be sent to the board members in advance so that board meeting time may be conserved and discussion time focused on questions that the board has about the material. On those occasions in which the subject matter is too sensitive to put on paper, the presentation

will be discussed at the meeting.

Committee matters

22 Number, structure and independence of committees
The current committee structure of the company seems appropriate. There will, from time to time, be occasions on which the board may want to form a new committee or disband a current committee depending upon the circumstances. The current six committees are audit, capital stock, director affairs, finance, executive compensation and public policy. The committee membership, with the exception of the finance committee, will consist only of independent directors as stipulated in Bylaw 2.12.

23 Assignment and rotation of committee members
The committee on director affairs is responsible, after consultation with the chief executive officer and with consideration of the desires of individual board members, for the assignment of board members to various committees.

It is the sense of the board that consideration should be given to rotating committee members periodically at about a five-year interval, but the board does not feel that such a rotation should be mandated as a policy since there may be reasons at a given point in time to maintain an individual director's committee membership for a longer period.

24 Frequency and length of committee meetings
The committee chairman, in consultation with committee members, will determine the frequency and length of the meetings of the committee.

25 Committee agenda
The chairman of the committee, in consultation with the appropriate members of management and staff, will develop the committee's agenda.

Each committee will issue a schedule of agenda subjects to be discussed for the ensuing year at the beginning of each year (to the degree these can be foreseen). This forward agenda will also be shared with the board.

Leadership development

26 Formal evaluation of the chief executive officer
The full board (outside directors) should make this evaluation annually, and it should be communicated to the chief executive officer by the (non-executive) chairman of the board or the lead director.

The evaluation should be based on objective criteria including performance of the business, accomplishment of long-term strategic objectives, development of management, etc.

The evaluation will be used by the executive compensation committee in the course of its deliberations when considering the compensation of the chief executive officer.

27 Succession planning
There should be an annual report by the chief executive officer to the board on succession planning.

There should also be available, on a continuing basis, the chief executive officer's recommendation as to a successor should he/she be unexpectedly disabled.

28 Management development
There should be an annual report to the board by the chief executive officer on the company's programme for management development.

This report should be given to the board at the same time as the succession planning report noted previously.

Grateful thanks are extended to the chairman and the board of General Motors for permission to reproduce these board guidelines.

4 Board effectiveness review checklist

There is no board of directors or governing body in the world which, if the members think about it, cannot improve its effectiveness. This is the belief behind this checklist of opportunities. All too readily board members grow old together. Often the business outgrows the board. Few boards take a rigorous look at themselves. A review of board effectiveness can be a salutary experience, but it can lead to important changes.

A board review involves a comprehensive and tough-minded look at the board and its activities. The aim is to explore the board's structure, style and processes in the light of changing company needs, to highlight potential problems for the future and provide the basis for improving effectiveness today.

Such a review needs the enthusiastic support and co-operation of all board members if it is to succeed. It can be led by the chairman, one of the outside directors, an *ad hoc* board committee or someone with suitable experience from outside the board. It is obviously a highly confidential activity.

The review process involves marshalling a lot of information about the underlying governance power-base in the company, the board structure and its members, and the way the board and its committees work, including the information they receive and the way they allocate their time. Various ideas, issues and opinions will then emerge. Alternatives can be developed and evaluated. In due course the options can be discussed by the directors, leading eventually to a strategy for the development of the board and the way it works. The process needs to be taken step by step.

1 Set the board review in the context of the company's business strategy

As companies grow in complexity, diversity and size, it seems obvious that their boards ought also to evolve to reflect such changes. Unfortunately this is not always the case. If, for example, the company's strategy involves new technologies, markets or international locations, if it is developing new strategic alliance or acquisition strategies, or if its plans call for alternative global financing strategies such as the use of derivatives, it is essential that among the board members are those able to understand the issues and, in due course, monitor executive management's performance. Thus the first step towards creating a strategy for board development is to consider the implications at board level of the corporate business strategy as a whole. The board review must be in line with, and preferably part of, the company's overall business strategy.

2 Review overall governance
This can be particularly important, yet easily overlooked. The key question is: who has ultimate power over the company and might this change over the strategic time horizon of the board review? If so, what would be the implications for governance and the board? For example, in a public listed company what are the prospects of a change of ownership through a friendly or hostile bid? Or in a company with a dominant shareholder, what might happen to the board if this shareholding changed hands? In a family firm, how might the balance of power change on succession? It is important not only to know precisely the current ownership of the voting equity, but also to consider possible future scenarios. Detailed knowledge of the company's articles of association is important as well. There may be unexpected clauses about percentages of shareholder votes needed to approve various strategic changes, such as introducing new capital or divesting part of the business.

3 Consider relevant external factors
This means looking at the context in which the governance of the company must operate over

the time horizon of the review. Are there any legal, political or societal factors that could affect the governance of the company? Examples include possible changes to company legislation in any of the countries in which the company operates, new regulations from the European Union about worker representation in strategic decision-making, the imposition of new disclosure requirements in the stock exchange listing rules, or the possible effects of a change of government. Any plans for developing the board must take account of the changing governance environment.

4 Review board structure

Consider the size of the board. Is it appropriate for the task that needs to be done? There may be a case for additional members; on the other hand, the board may have grown too big. Consider the structure of the board. Is the balance between executive and non-executive members appropriate? This issue will have to be reviewed along with the identification of board style and the way the members work together. Are enough of the non-executive directors genuinely independent? This means ensuring that the independent outside directors have no relationships with the company that could affect the exercise of genuinely objective judgment. Are the posts of chairman of the board and chief executive separate? Is the present arrangement the most satisfactory for the future?

5 Identify board style

Consider how the board's work has evolved in recent years. Reflect on the effects of changes in chairman and other members. Review the way the directors work together. Is this a genuinely professional board style or are there elements of the rubber stamp, the representative board or the country club? What changes might be necessary to meet different circumstances that may arise in the future?

6 Review board membership and formulate succession plans

Consider the detailed membership of the board. Summarise the resume of each director. Does the board have the balance of knowledge, skills and experience that will be needed for the planned future of the company? Look at the age profile of members. How many directors will retire over the review's time horizon? What is the probability of any directors resigning? Develop succession plans for both executive and non-executive directors. Boards should always have a portfolio of potential non-executive directors who could be considered for board appointment, and the management development plans for senior executive staff should also include their potential as directors.

7 Consider director development and training

As much attention should be given to director development and training as is given to management development and training, but it seldom is. Directors all too readily assume that, having reached the board, they must have the experience to perform as directors. But governance, the work of the board, is not the same as management. It calls for additional knowledge and different skills. Consider the development needs of each director. This could involve a carefully devised induction or updating programme on the company and its work; or building up experience by, for example, chairing a board task force or one of the board committees; or it might be achieved through participation in the growing number of director-level courses and programmes around the world.

8 Achieving greater efficiency: review directors' time and information

How does the board spend its time? Is this the most effective use of one of the most valuable resources the company has? Does the board delegate some of its work to board committees

and are these as effective as they could be? This
information can be extracted from an analysis of
the agenda and minutes of the board and its
committees, and by discussing the issue with
each director. Similarly, review the nature, extent
and adequacy of the information available to
directors. How could the routing of board papers
be improved? Can directors readily obtain the
additional information they want? Do the outside
directors have access to management
information? Is there a case for board-level
briefings to keep directors up to date and
provide the context for board-level discussions?
What ideas does each director have for
improvement in the information process?

9 Achieving greater effectiveness: better strategy formulation and policy-making

Review the board's contribution to the
performance roles of strategy formulation and
policy-making. Is adequate time devoted to this
part of the board's responsibilities? Are all board
members adequately informed about strategic
matters? Is there a shared vision and
understanding of the company's core values and
competences among all the directors? Are there
any differences of view as to the strategic
direction of the firm? Are the policy guidelines
laid down by the board adequate for
management decision-making, balancing control
and freedom appropriately? What ideas do
directors have for improvement?

10 Achieving greater effectiveness: better executive supervision and accountability

Turning to the conformance roles of the board,
do the directors adequately monitor and
supervise executive management? Is the
feedback of information relevant and timely?
How might the process be improved? Seek the
opinions of all directors and senior managers,
also the auditors and others in a position to take
a view on board activities. Is the board providing
appropriate accountability to all those with a

legitimate claim to be informed? Does this include a commitment to employees, customers and suppliers, or does the board accept a responsibility to be accountable only to the shareholders? Is this responsibility adequately fulfilled? Consider the published report, other communications and meetings with the members, analysts and the media. What ideas are there for improvement?

11 Develop and agree the strategy for board development

From the mass of hard data, opinion and ideas for improvement that have been gathered, marshal the facts, identify alternatives and articulate their implications. Develop a report for discussion by the board. To encourage open discussion and creativity such a review might well take place as part of a strategy seminar, rather than in a formal board meeting. Move towards developing a strategy for developing the board. This could include planned changes to board size, structure or membership, new sources and forms of providing information, alternative uses of directors' time (such as a new committee structure), alternative formats for board meetings, or calling on some directors to commit different amounts of time to their board duties. Agree the strategy, ensuring that it is consistent with, indeed part of, the overall business strategy.

12 Determine action plans and projects

Finally, develop the procedures, plans and projects that will turn the strategy into realised change. Ensure commitment from all those involved. Get feedback periodically to confirm that the changes are taking place as planned and that the results are as expected. Continue the strategic review and programme for change as part of the board's constant learning and relearning process.

5 An induction checklist for directors

Outside directors never know enough about the business to be useful and inside directors always know too much to be independent. So runs one criticism of traditional board practice. Working through the items on this checklist will improve the quality of directors' contributions and reduce the time it takes for them to contribute fully and effectively. Induction exercises for directors will ensure that all board members are fully informed about the company, the business and its financials, the three fundamental areas in which directors need to be conversant and competent. Directors vary in the extent of their knowledge of the company and its business, but the checklist will provide an *aide memoire* for both outside and inside directors.

The checklist can be used by chairmen and CEOs planning an induction programme for their board members, as well as by newly appointed directors wanting to brief themselves. Many of the questions are ones they should ask before accepting a directorship. The checklist has also proved useful for directors of long standing, by highlighting areas of knowledge and work that they might previously have overlooked.

1 KNOWLEDGE OF THE COMPANY

The first broad focus of the induction programme is on the company and its governance. The chairman, other long-serving directors and the company secretary can often be very helpful in this regard. If in doubt, it is always wise to seek legal opinion.

Ownership power

In the joint stock limited liability company ownership is the ultimate basis of governance power. What is the balance of the equity shareholding and voting power? Has the balance changed in the past and how have the votes been used? How might it change and the voting strength be used in the future? Consider, in a family company, for example, what might happen as shares are transferred on succession. Or, in a widely held public company, consider the potential for a merger or hostile bid. What anti-takeover provisions, if any, are in place? How effective might they be?

In a company limited by guarantee, or any other corporate entity governed by its members, how active is the membership in governance matters? Could this situation change in the future? Explore the way that the board communicates with the members and whether there have been any attempts by members to influence corporate affairs. Non-profit organisations often seem to generate controversial, even adversarial, member activity.

Rules, regulations and company law
Study the articles of association and memorandum or corporate rule book. These are the formal documents created on incorporation and updated subject to the approval of the members. Within the constraints of the company law and the listing rules (for a quoted public company), they determine the way the company can be governed. The memorandum, for example, could limit the size of the board, lay down rules for the selection of the board chairman, or define conditions for the meeting and voting of the members. All too often directors are not familiar with the contents of the company's memorandum and are surprised to find themselves constrained in some way, for example, in the percentage of members' votes needed to change the capital structure or sell off part of the enterprise.

In a listed public company be familiar with the listing rules of the stock exchanges on which the company's shares are quoted. Some directors feel that this is a matter that can reasonably be left to the company secretary, share registrar or corporate legal counsel. But it is difficult for people not familiar with the basic requirements to ask appropriate questions that ensure compliance. There is an important distinction between delegation and abdication of responsibility.

Be familiar with the broad scope of the company law of the jurisdiction in which the company is incorporated and has its major bases. Obviously the detailed requirements of company law vary between Delaware and California, Australia and Canada, or the UK and France, but there can also be fundamental differences, particularly in the handling of private companies. Companies incorporated in the British Virgin Islands, for example, are not required to have an audit, there is virtually no public filing of documents and the rights of members can be severely limited if they are not also directors.

It is not necessary for a director to be a lawyer or an accountant to fulfil such responsibilities, but company law around the world typically expects directors to show the degree of knowledge and skill that a reasonable person would associate with company directorship. In the old days this might not have amounted to very much; today expectations are running high.

Board structure, membership and processes

What is the structure of the board? In other words, what is the balance between executive and non-executive directors? In your opinion is this appropriate? Are the outside, non-executive directors independent, or do they have some connection with the company such as being a nominee for a major shareholder or lender, being members of the family of the chairman or CEO, or holding an executive directorship in the past? Such matters could affect your assessment of the position they take on board issues.

Is the board chairmanship separated from the role of chief executive? If not, is there a danger that the board is dominated by a single individual, and are you able to operate in such a climate? Who are the other board members? Do you know them? If not, some effort to learn about their background, experience and reputation could reinforce your early contributions to board discussions. Meeting individual directors to discuss corporate matters before your first board meeting might help you to discover whether the chemistry of the board is likely to be appropriate for you. Is there a succession plan for key directors and top management? Is there a strategy for development at board level to ensure that the business does not outgrow the board?

How often does the board meet? How long do typical meetings last? What role does the chairman play in board matters? Ask for the agenda and minutes of recent board meetings. Talk to the company secretary about the way the board meetings are run. Does the board operate with committees – an executive committee, audit, remuneration or nominating committees, for example? Find out what you can about the membership, chairmanship and style of these committees. Study their minutes and discuss with their chairman or the company secretary how they operate.

What information do the directors routinely receive? Ask for all the documentation provided for recent meetings. Study the reports and consider the scope of the routine performance data provided. Is it adequate? Does the board have briefings and presentations from non-board senior executives or other experts from time to time? Do the directors meet the auditors periodically?

2 KNOWLEDGE OF THE BUSINESS
The second focus of this induction checklist is on the business itself. Do you know enough about the business to make an effective contribution? This is a reasonable question to ask an outside director who has little or no experience in this particular industry. Interestingly, it is also a pertinent question to put to many executive

directors. Expertise and success in a particular function (finance and accounting, perhaps) or high managerial performance in running a division or group company, does not necessarily provide a view of the business as a whole. Indeed, it might have created a narrow window of experience through which the entire corporate business is viewed. This part of the checklist is again relevant to all directors.

The basic business processes

Can you outline the fundamental steps in the added-value chain or network of the firm? This is as pertinent a question for directors of a bank, a telecommunications company or an airline, as it is for those of a manufacturing business (although the basic processes are often more difficult to identify). Are you familiar with the major sources of the business inputs, where they come from and who provides them? Within the business processes, which add the value and provide competitive advantage and which drive the costs? What are the core competences or capabilities of the business? What is the range of products and services provided by the business? Find out all you can from catalogues, trade literature, customer promotions, trade shows and similar sources of information. Who are the customers? What sectors and markets are served? Pareto's law often applies to products and customers: 80% of the value comes from 20% of the list. Which products and customers form this 20%?

Corporate strategies

Does the firm have a written mission statement or a set of core values? Is there a shared view of the business direction, clearly articulated in strategies, plans and projects? Obtain copies, discuss them with the chairman or CEO. If not, what is the broad direction of the business; what strategies are evident from recent actions, such as strategies of growth through investment in new product development or through acquisition and divestment? Are there any written policies or management manuals? Study and discuss them. For example, as far as customers are concerned, are there specific pricing policies and credit policies?

Who are the principal competitors? What competitive advantages and disadvantages do they have and what strategies are they pursuing? Are there potential entrants into the market or technological developments, products or services that might provide new competition? Is the business involved in strategic alliances; for example, joint ventures to develop new strategic areas, to supply goods or services, or provide access to distribution channels?

How is strategic change initiated in the firm? Does the board respond to ideas put forward by the CEO and top management, or is the board intimately involved in strategy formulation?

Organisation, management and people

What is the formal organisation structure? Discuss with the CEO and other members of top management how the organisation works in practice. Form a view of the management culture and style throughout the business: it may differ around the world.

What management control systems are used, such as budgetary planning and control, profit centres, performance centres and so on? What management performance measures are used? Are they linked to managerial incentives? Are there employee or top management share-option schemes?

How many employees are there in the various parts of the business? What are the characteristics of the workforce? Are trade unions important and is there a policy towards them? What are the remuneration and other employment policies?

Overall, how would you assess the current position of the business? What needs to be done to maintain and enhance future performance?

3 KNOWLEDGE OF THE FINANCIALS

Finally, we turn to a sector which inevitably features strongly in typical board discussions: the financial aspects.

Study the annual accounts and directors' reports for the past few years. What have been the trends?

Consider the trends of key financial ratios, for example: overall performance ratios, such as return on equity and return on investment; and working capital management ratios, such as inventory turnover rates, liquidity ratios, debt collection rates.

Trends are likely to convey more information than the actual ratios for the business itself, whereas the financial ratios at a point in time can be useful for cross-industry comparisons. What are the future projections for these financial criteria? How does the financial position of the company compare with that of its key competitors?

Review the financial performance of parts of the business, such as product or geographical divisions or subsidiary companies. Review the criteria used in investment project appraisals.

How is the company financed? What is the financial structure? What implications might the debt:equity ratio have for the future? For example, what might be the effect of a significant change in interest rates given this gearing or leverage?

Who are the auditors? Ask to see the any "management letter" written after the last audit discussing any issues that arose during the audit.

4 EXPECTATIONS ON APPOINTMENT

All directors should discuss with the chairman what is expected of their directorship before accepting nomination. Consequently, a crucial part of any induction briefing should review the expectations of the chairman and the other directors.

Is a specific role expected of you? Was there a special reason, perhaps, why you were nominated for the board? For example, did the nomination reflect your particular knowledge in some area, or that you would bring special skills or experience to board discussions, or provide a special channel of communication and information? Or was the nomination made because of your overall experience and potential contribution to all aspects of the board's work? Are you capable of fulfilling these expectations? If not, what other information, knowledge, skill will you need to obtain?

How much time are you expected to give to the board, its committees and to other aspects of the company's affairs? This should cover not only attendance at regular meetings, but the time needed for briefings and discussions, visits within the company and preparation. Outside directors will have to ensure that this is compatible with other demands on their time. Executive directors will need to harmonise these expectations and their director responsibilities with the duties required under their contracts of employment with the company.

Although all directors have the right to be informed on all board matters, confirm that you will have appropriate access to the information you require. This should cover not only formal board papers, but also the right to seek additional information if necessary. Are you able to talk to the members of management? If so, under what circumstances?

Last, but not least, review the details of the contractual relationship between you and the company. Is there a written contract or a formal letter of appointment from the chairman? What are the terms of appointment as a director? Length of appointment? Terms and likelihood of reappointment? Basis of the remuneration package and manner of review? Terms of any director and officers' indemnity insurance (particularly important in the increasingly litigious climate in which directors in many parts of the world have to operate)?

Finally, a word of encouragement. All

directors, without exception, face a challenge as they join a new board. Effective board membership involves a learning experience. It should start well before the director attends the first board meeting and should continue during all the rest. The successful director is the one who can say: "Aha! I hadn't realised that, now I understand," not once but continuously, throughout his or her service to the board.

6 Case studies

METALLGESELLSCHAFT: INSIGHTS INTO THE TWO-TIER BOARD

Metallgesellschaft (MG) is a major group of companies incorporated and listed in Germany. In 1994 massive losses from exposure to trading in oil derivatives were incurred by the German group's US subsidiary MG Corporation. In the US oil-trading operations, customers were offered long-term fixed-rate contracts for the supply of oil products. Many customers were keen to lock in at prices that were low after the Gulf war. MG could have hedged its exposure to subsequent oil price rises by buying forward contracts of the same maturity as its commitment to supply oil. Instead it appears to have bought shorter-dated oil derivative contracts, rolling them over on maturity. This could have proved profitable but the hedging mismatch left the company vulnerable to a widening of the spread between short- and long-term oil prices. The worst happened. Spot oil prices fell when OPEC failed to reduce production in autumn 1993. The long-term rates failed to reflect the movements of the short-term rates and MG's exposure became apparent.

The German Shareholder Protection Group DSW called for a special inquiry into the Metallgesellschaft supervisory board and the Frankfurt prosecutor's office began an official inquiry. Why did the normal supervisory board checks and balances mechanism fail to stop this exposure? Did the supervisory board even know about these risks? Did the management board keep the supervisory board properly informed? More fundamentally, the question has been raised as to whether the German approach to corporate governance should be replaced by the Anglo-Saxon unitary board, with executive and non-executive directors working together to direct and control the company, with responsibilities for ensuring both business performance and conformance.

Speaking to the *Financial Times* (February 8th 1994) Ms Schneider-Lenné, a member of the Deutsche Bank management board as well as a non-executive director of the British company ICI, said that German companies could learn from the best Anglo-Saxon corporate governance practices. "Whereas German supervisory boards normally meet no more than four times a year, UK boards – including the non-executive directors – tend to meet ten times a year."

A DM3 billion recapitalisation rescue package was proposed by the group's lead banker Deutsche Bank, involving scores of other financial houses. In the event the deadline was missed and the shares were suspended. The sale of non-core subsidiaries was also proposed. Questions were asked about the propriety of banks holding dominant shareholdings and being represented on supervisory boards. Does this not hold potential for a conflict of interest? For example, did the restructuring proposals of Metallgesellschaft favour shareholders over other creditors?

According to John Craven, the only non-German member of the MG management board, in an interview with the *Financial Times* (February 18th 1994), 65% of the equity was held by five institutions including two banks. "There is a community of interest between shareholders and creditors to keep the group trading. The perception that the banks in Germany have a disproportionate influence over the affairs of German companies and exercise this through the many memberships of corporate supervisory boards ... is a wrong perception. German corporate law states that the responsibility of the members of the board of managing directors (the *Vorstand*) and that of the supervisory board (the *Aufsichtsrat*) is to look after the interest of all the stakeholders in the business. This extends not only to the interest of the shareholders and the creditor banks, but also to the interests of the company as a going concern and to the interests of the suppliers, the customers, the workforce, the management and the communities in which the company operates."

German companies have been reluctant to seek funds on the international, predominantly US, financial markets because they did not want to make the financial disclosures required under GAAP (generally accepted accounting principles). Daimler-Benz, Germany's biggest industrial company, did so in 1994 but in the process redefined a reported profit under German rules of DM168m as a loss under GAAP rules of DM949m. Analysts suggest that more German companies might come to the international markets subsequently.

However, for many this would require a fundamental shift from the German collaborative structure of governance to the Anglo-Saxon confrontational equity culture. Such a conversion of German attitudes does not seem likely in the short term. It is true that some convergence of corporate governance is being encouraged by the globalisation of business, particularly in the financial field, by the worldwide coordination of the securities regulators (IOSCO) and by the growing acceptance of International Accounting Standards. But the time is not yet ripe for convergence in corporate governance.

Similarly, we are unlikely to see German governance processes replace the supervisory board with the unitary board. The MG case probably reflects personal and procedural failures in specific circumstances. It no more illustrates the failure of the two-tier concept than the fate of the Maxwell group in the UK demonstrates the limitations of the unitary board.

SAATCHI AND SAATCHI: INSIGHTS INTO CORPORATE GOVERNANCE FROM DIFFERENT PERSPECTIVES

The case of Saatchi and Saatchi shows the current lack of an overall conceptual framework for corporate governance.

Early in 1994 the Chicago-based investment

fund Harris Associates, led by fund manager David Herro, began to acquire a significant stake in the London-based international advertising firm Saatchi and Saatchi. With a stake approaching 10%, Mr Herro felt able to write to the company suggesting that changes were necessary at the top. "The company needs a chairman who will be more complementary to and compatible with the chief executive," he wrote. The chairman of Saatchi and Saatchi at that time was Maurice Saatchi, co-founder with his brother Charles. The chief executive was Charles Scott. The board decided against taking any action on the suggestion from Mr Herro, who then began to organise opposition to the chairman at the shareholders' annual meeting to be held in June 1994.

At the board meeting in May 1994 some non-executive directors were persuaded that Maurice Saatchi should be asked to stand down. But a few directors flew over to see Mr Herro, who agreed that he could be given a "final chance". At the board meeting in December 1994 directors were even more concerned. A share-option package had been proposed for Maurice Saatchi that many felt would not be well received by the shareholders, who had seen their share price collapse in recent years.

Mr Herro, who by this time had the support of a number of US funds, was now joined by UK fund manager M&G Securities. The company's financial advisers, S.G. Warburg and UBS Securities, felt that if it came to a shareholder vote, the chairman would not survive. On December 16th 1994 the board voted for the removal of Maurice Saatchi as chairman.

Early in January 1995 Maurice Saatchi and his brother Charles sold their 1.8m shares in the company. A few days later three top executives of the firm resigned. Maurice Saatchi announced plans to set up a rival agency with those who had just resigned. Writs and counter-writs ensued. Three major clients of Saatchi & Saatchi, British Airways, Dixon's Electrical and the Mirror

Group, withdrew their business from the company.

In 1987 the Saatchi and Saatchi share price had stood at over £50. Subsequent losses had brought it down to £1.54 by December 1994. By mid-January, following the above saga, it was down to 95 pence. A year later the price was still around that level.

Proponents of **stewardship theory**, which underpins the company law perspective, might argue that these events illustrate a rediscovery of the original 19th century concept of the corporation in which ownership is the basis of power. In exercising this shareholder power, the institutional investors were acting as proprietors rather than punters. Recent examples of the similar use of institutional investor power in the USA had unseated the chairmen of IBM, General Motors and American Express. Can the actions by a group of institutional investors really be presented as shareholder democracy, when the rest of the shareholders have not been consulted? We do not know whether the shareholders agreed; they were not asked. Certainly their investment has not benefited in the short term.

Lord King, chairman of British Airways, raised another issue about the relationship of institutional investors with top management when he argued that institutional investors had "highjacked the corporate governance process". (*Financial Times* January 15th 1995)

Stakeholder theorists could have a field day with this case. Neither shareholders nor management should be the sole arbiters of power over the corporation, they would argue. The case shows the significance of accountability to other stakeholders, including the employees, the providers of non-equity capital and, particularly, the clients. They would present the case, not as an issue of management versus institutional investors, nor as a clash between creative and financially oriented people, but as a question of who should exercise power over the modern international group of businesses. Who should be accountable to whom, and for what?

Agency theory provides an unambiguous perspective, one that would be readily shared by most economists and some legal theoreticians. The directors of the company are the agents for their principals, the shareholders. Agents will inevitably seek to maximise their own utility, within the bounds of the transaction costs involved. The case provides a simple example. The flow of information and the workings of the market will ensure that the interests of the various investors are met, even though they may not be homogeneous.

By contrast the proponents of **role theory** might point out the significance of the key parts played by the actors in this drama. A theoretical explanation which fails to include the strikingly different perspectives and personalities of Maurice Saatchi, Charles Scott and David Herro surely cannot pretend to be authoritative. We are dealing with real people, not the abstractions of stewardship, stakeholder or agency theories. Their self-perceptions, their view of the situation and their values matter.

A **post-modern perspective** would probably use the data to illustrate the continuous discontinuity, destabilisation and chaos that marks the shift from the modern world, in which science, rationality and reason prevailed, as typified by socio-philosophical structures, systems and constructs, into the post-modern world in which reasons have replaced Reason, with horizontal networks displacing hierarchy and centrality.

Much of the theorising in the corporate governance field to date has been unfettered by considerations of the players themselves, just as Karl Marx assumed that people were in the grip of the forces of capitalism outside their individual control, and Adam Smith depicted man as a rational, utility-maximiser in an efficient market.

7 Sources of information

Australian Institute of Company Directors
3F, 71 York Street
Sydney, NSW 2000
Australia

Tel: +61 2 299 8788
Fax: +61 2 299 1008

The Australian Institute of Company Directors
(CD), admits as fellows directors and alternate
directors and as members senior executives with
responsibilities equivalent to an executive
director, partners in professional practices and
academics at professorial level. It publishes a
journal and runs director development
programmes.

**Corporate Governance – an international
review**
Blackwell Publishers
108 Cowley Road
Oxford, OX4 1JF
UK

Tel: +44 1865 791 100
Fax: +44 1865 191 347

238 Main Street
Suite 501
Cambridge, MA 02142
USA

Tel: +1 617 547 7110
Fax: +1 617 547 0789

A quarterly academic and professional
publication devoted to issues in corporate
governance and board effectiveness with current
developments, research, reports and cases from
around the world.
   For further information see
http://www.blackwellpublishers.co.uk

Institute of Directors

116 Pall Mall
London SW1Y 5ED

Tel: +44 171 730 4600
Fax: +44 171 930 1949

The Institute of Directors (IOD) has a membership of some 33,000 individuals in the UK and EU who serve on boards of all sizes. There are IOD members on 750 of *The Times* Top 1,000 companies, with over 60% of members being from medium-sized and small companies. The IOD publishes *The Director* (see below) as well as guidelines on good practice.

The Centre for Director Development at the Institute of Directors

116 Pall Mall
London SW1Y 5ED

Tel: +44 171 839 1233
Fax: +44 171 930 1949

The Centre for Director Development is an authority on director training and provides a range of director development services, including courses, workshops and short updates at various centres and on an in-company basis. It also offers a Diploma in Company Direction which provides an opportunity to be assessed and accredited against a national standard.

The Director

Director Publications
Mountbarrow House
Elizabeth Street
London SW1W 9RB

Tel: +44 171 730 6060
Fax: +44 171 235 5627

A monthly journal for directors.

Lens
Suite 601, 13th Street
Washington, DC 20005
USA

Tel: +1 202 783 3348
Fax: +1 202 783 3316

On-line corporate governance material, a source
of bibliographical data on the World Wide Web.
 For further information see LENS WWW home
page or info@lens-inc.com

National Association of Corporate Directors
Suite 560
1701 L Street, NW
Washington, DC 20036
USA

Tel: +1 202 775 0509

The mission of the National Association of
Corporate Directors (NACD) is to enhance the
governance and performance of business entities.
Since its founding in 1977 it has pursued this
goal by offering a broad spectrum of educational
and membership benefits, including publications,
seminars and consultative services. The Directors'
Register records those seeking appointments. The
NACD holds an annual corporate governance
review, where it presents the Director of the Year
Award.

University of New England
Armidale, NSW 2351
Australia

Tel: +61 67 732480
Fax: +61 67 733204

The university has run The Company Director's
Course for some years, which can be taken as a
residential programme, in courses in conjunction
with other universities and by distance learning.

8 Recommended reading list

The Accounting Standards Steering Committee, *The Corporate Report* – a discussion paper published for comment, Moorgate Place, London, 1975.

Barney, Jay B., "The Debate between Traditional Management Theory and Organisational Economics – substantive differences or inter-group conflict?", *The Academy of Management Review*, Vol. 15, No. 3, July 1990. A discussion of agency and stewardship theories.

Berle, A. and Means, G., *The Modern Corporation and Private Property*, Macmillan, New York, 1932. The first and most frequently quoted study of corporate governance.

Bosch, Henry, *The Director at Risk – accountability in the boardroom*, Pitman Publishing, Australia, 1995.

Cadbury, Sir Adrian (chairman), *The Report of the Committee on the Financial Aspects of Corporate Governance*, Gee and Co, London, 1992.

Cochran, Philip L. and Wartick, Steven L., *Corporate Governance – a review of the literature*, Financial Executives Research Foundation, Morristown, New Jersey, 1988.

Demb, Ada and Neubauer, Fred, *The Corporate Board – confronting the paradoxes*, Oxford University Press, New York, 1992.

Fama, Eugene and Jensen, Michael, "Separation of Ownership and Control", *Journal of Law and Economics*, Vol. 26, June 1983. A classic on agency theory.

Greenbury, Sir Richard (chairman), *The Report of the Committee on Directors' Remuneration*, Gee and Co, London, 1995.

Handy, Charles, "What is a company for?", *Corporate Governance – an international review*, Vol. 1, No. 1, January 1993.

Hilmer, Frederick G. (chairman), *Strictly Ballroom – improving governance to enrich company performance*, a study facilitated by The Sydney Institute, Information Australia, Melbourne, VIC, Australia, 1993.

Hilmer Frederick G. and Tricker, Robert I., "Board effectiveness", in *The Australian Company Director's Handbook*, Australian Institute of Company Directors, Sydney, Australia 1991.

Lufkin, Joseph C.F. and Gallagher, David, *International Corporate Governance*, Euromoney Books, London, 1990.

Millstein, Ira M. and Katsch, Salem M., *The Limits of Corporate Power – existing constraints on the exercise of corporate discretion*, Collier-Macmillan, New York, 1981.

Monks, Robert A.G. and Minow, Nell, *Power and Accountability*, HarperCollins, New York, 1991.

Monks, Robert A.G. and Minow, Nell, *Corporate Governance*, Blackwell, Oxford, 1994.

Ohmae, Kenichi, *The Mind of the Strategist*, Penguin, London, 1986.

Porter, Michael, *Competitive Strategy*, Basic Books, New York, 1980.

Porter, Michael, *Competitive Advantage*, Basic Books, New York, 1985.

Spencer, Anne, *On the Edge of the Organisation – the role of the outside director*, Wiley, London, 1983.

Sun Tse, *The Art of War*, Bamboo sticks, c. 600 BC. Available in an number of English translations and commentaries.

Taylor, B. and Tricker, R.I., *The Director's Manual*, Director Books, London, 1990.

Tricker, R.I., *Corporate Governance*, Gower, Aldershot, 1984.

Tricker, R.I., *International Corporate Governance – text, readings and cases*, Prentice Hall, Singapore, 1994.